HOUSE ON A BUDGET

Making Smart Choices to Build the Home You Want

DUO DICKINSON, AIA

Photography by Ken Gutmaker

The Taunton Press

To William Raub, who left this life the day this book was born: 9/11/01

This book is published under the joint imprint of The American Institute of Architects and
The Taunton Press, Inc.

THE AMERICAN INSTITUTE OF ARCHITECTS

The American Institute of Architects, founded in 1857, is a professional society of architects with
over 70,000 members in the United States and abroad. Through its national, regional, state, and local
components, the AIA works to achieve more humane built environments and higher standards of
professionalism for architects through education, government advocacy, community redevelopment,
and public outreach activities. AIA's website is located at aia.org.

AIA, The American Institute of Architects, and the AIA logo are registered trademarks and service marks
of The American Institute of Architects.

The Taunton Press
Inspiration for hands-on living®

The Taunton Press, Inc., 63 South Main Street, PO Box 5506, Newtown, CT 06470-5506
e-mail: tp@taunton.com

House on a Budget was originally published in hardcover in 2004 by The Taunton Press, Inc., as *The House
You Build*.

Editor: Peter Chapman
Interior design and layout: Lori Wendin
Illustrator: Vincent Babak
Photographer: Ken Gutmaker

Library of Congress Cataloging-in-Publication Data
Dickinson, Duo.
  The house you build : making real-world choices to get the home you want / Duo Dickinson.
    .p. cm.
  ISBN-13: 978-1-56158-616-5 hardcover
  ISBN-10: 1-56158-616-1 hardcover
  ISBN-13: 978-1-56158-923-4 paperback (with flaps)
  ISBN-10: 1-56158-923-3 paperback (with flaps)
  1. Architecture, Domestic--United States--Designs and plans. 2. Architecture--United States--
20th century--Designs and plans. 3. Architecture--United States--21st century--Designs and plans.
4. Architect-designed houses--United States. 5. Building--Economic aspects. I. Title.
  NA7208.D53 2004
  728'.37--dc22
                        2004003604
Printed in Singapore
10 9 8 7 6 5 4 3 2 1

The following manufacturers/names appearing in *House on a Budget* are trademarks: Dryvit®, IKEA®,
Kynar®, TJI®

Acknowledgments

●●● Of the six books I've written, this one has been by far the most aggressively researched, reviewed, and edited. The Taunton Press, publisher Jim Childs in particular, has layered perspective and focus on the book from the beginning without smothering its basic premise. It's a book that hasn't been written before, so it has risks for a publisher, and I am grateful that Taunton is willing to take those risks.

Thanks must first be given to the architects who were selected for publication—they are among the finest practitioners anywhere—and to their clients, the homeowners who are the very constituency this book is written for. Without the art of photographer Ken Gutmaker, the architects' work and my words would have a paler presence.

There's risk for any architect trying to write. Beyond embarrassment, there's the risk of losing your practice to make a point. My office has had to keep the 40 "other" jobs together as I sat at the laptop. My thanks go to Mark Allen, Ed Fusco, Jonathan Gibbs, Michael Landino, Howard Needler, Nikki Riccio, Jesus Rivera, Doug Simpson, Ariel Torres, and Jim Wilson for their patience and willingness to pick up the slack—although I fear my distraction may have been a welcome relief for them. Similarly my family, Liz, Will, and Sam, have all given support to a project that has imposed itself on day-to-day life for several years.

In the end, two people made this book a reality. Peter Chapman is the best editor I have ever worked with; his unrelenting reality checks mean that you, dear reader, do not have to suffer the likes of *architectonic, rendered, constructivist,* or other architectural buzzwords. Beyond all others, Cheryl Alison was boundless in her positive focus, intelligent intercession, and God-given skill of turning mumbled musings into the English language. I could not have written this book, nor the two that preceded it, without her gifts and guts.

⋮ Contents

Introduction :

EVERYBODY WANTS TWO THINGS FOR THEIR HOME: that it be beautiful and on budget. Most people spend more for the place where they live than any other physical object they will ever own. But compared to almost any other retail transaction, homebuyers usually have the least control over what they get. The result? High stakes purchasing + low expectations = frustrating reality. But this reality is absent from almost all media portrayals, academic exercises, or the tradition of professional home design, where money is assumed to be readily available for great designs.

There are plenty of books on cost meant for builders, developers, and economists (with all the visual appeal of a calculus textbook), and there are unending parades of visually seductive and energizing images of homes on television, in the movies, and in print, but those images have no price tags attached to them. This book breaks down the unspoken barrier between beautiful homes and their budgets. I know of no other book that takes on this disconnect.

To break through 50 years of denial, an extensive search netted hundreds of houses that triumphed over their crisply defined budgets. From that pool, 19 homes were chosen for publication. The criteria for selection were as follows:

- The homes had to be full-time residences built in the last eight years (no renovations). One vacation home was so compelling that we decided to include it.

- The cost of construction of these homes had to be competitive with their spec-built counterparts for their region at the time of their construction. The comparison between spec houses and those in this

book is on a functional basis rather than by size or cost per square foot. Given the custom design of each home, they should "fit" their owner's needs, so overall size is not a criterion for comparison.

- The homes were not owner built; all had general contractors, or if the owner served as the general contractor, the vast majority of work and materials were purchased for market rate fees.

- Building, site development,and design fee costs were requested from all submitters, and most provided them. Site acquisition costs were not requested as the cost of land is so variable depending on location that any citation would serve more to confuse the reader than to provide useful information.

Books about contemporary architecture seldom, if ever, deal with costs, dates, clients, and levels of architectural service, but these facts are the central issues for anyone thinking about building a house. The inclusion of these data allows readers to get a clear sense that older and/or more rural projects may be viewed in an inordinately positive light and, conversely, the more recent and more urban projects may seem to be at a cost disadvantage to those in different circumstances.

Success in architecture is always subjective, but in this case all the owners and builders who were part of the projects submitted written statements describing their experiences. In every statement there was enthusiastic testimony of the project's ultimate success—even if there were some bumps in the road. In the end, these are human stories, replete with choices and foibles. A lot like life in general.

MATERIAL MIX. It's not the cost of the materials that makes a home special, it's the way they are organized, detailed, and finished. [facing page]

COMPOSITION. When carefully composed, windows, drywall, and natural wood make rooms that both embrace those living within and bring the outside in. [left]

THE BIG PICTURE. A simple house form, easy and inexpensive to build, makes a delightful architectural counterpoint to a wild site. [right]

Finding the Third Way

HOMEBUYERS IN AMERICA TEND TO LOOK AT HOUSES IN ONE OF TWO WAYS.

Surrounding us today is a sea of "production" housing, houses that are typically set in subdivisions, built en masse with generic materials to create the biggest house at the most appealing price point. Trying to be all things to all home-buyers, the typical American spec house is often oversized, underbuilt, and dressed up with a veneer of superficial features and materials intended to market the house rather than meet any particular need. Just like fast food, the new houses that most people can afford today satisfy only their most basic needs without giving real satisfaction.

The second window to the world of houses is found in the popular media where the "lifestyles of the rich and famous" are put on display. This is the flip side to the wholesale mediocrity surrounding us—fabulous houses that are paraded before hopeful housing consumers in magazines and on television. These houses express innovation, artful and evocative design, and enriching materials and features, but they are financially out of reach for all but the richest among us and are presented without any reference to their cost.

So people who want to shape their own homes are most often faced with readily available mediocrity or inaccessible fantasy. But there is a third way. Rather than limit your choices to what's already built or focus your

fantasies on media-celebrated dream homes, you can tackle your housing needs dead on. If you build your own home, you can control costs by being directly involved in the design and construction. This has not been the 20th-century American tradition, where new homes are marketed like any product, and your choices boil down to tweaking a stock plan with pre-determined "options."

To build your own home in a world where custom construction is assumed to be priced beyond the average homeowner's budget requires a savvy awareness of the opportunities and pitfalls that lie in the design and building world. This book seeks to provide that aware-ness by showing the myriad choices made in 19 separate house-building stories. The truth is that many people who think they have no viable housing options can build their own home if they know the impact of the choices they make—like building with modular compo-nents or opting for an inexpensive, less-than-perfect lot in an urban setting. Although it is the homeowner who ultimately makes his or

her dreams come true, architects dedicated to designing homes are a crucial gateway through which these choices can be researched and understood.

ARCHITECTS AND THE THIRD WAY

Responding to a growing number of homeowners who need their services, a small but growing group of architects find inspiration in the domestic dreams of their impassioned clients. Through diligence, resourcefulness, and some risk taking, homeowners are finding they can gain increased control of their home's design by partnering with professional home designers who share their values. While this approach clearly represents a small percentage of the houses being built in America today, I believe it points the way to the future of home design, particularly in light of the unprecedented growth in home ownership during the last generation.

More than anything else we own, homes offer the greatest risk of pushing us into bank-ruptcy, or more often inaction. It's usually impossible to overcome a price tag even

10 percent beyond a homebuyer's budget. If you hire an architect, that price tag has to include the architect's fee—and that means the homeowner needs to know what services are offered and what costs are involved. The examples in this book show how homeowners have made the tough choices that allow their homes to maximize their efficiency and the economics of generic building materials without compromising aesthetics. The custom-tailored homes built embracing this design ethic can be cost-competitive with their bloated spec counterparts—even when the cost of an architect's fee is included.

Without professional design skills to help make your home buildable, there is no viable alternative—no third way—to the easy, instant gratification of buying a spec box or the no-risk fantasizing over houses presented in the media. For the last 50 years, most housing consumers have either settled for a plan-book design they can live with or lamented the unfairness of a glossy image that turns out to cost three times what they can afford. There are architects who have the experience and integrity to evaluate budgets, sites, and desires before they are hired, thereby reality-checking dreams and limiting risk.

●●● **GOING WITH THE FLOW.** Painted drywall, wood, and a careful eye toward scale and the use of natural light can make the simplest of spaces (here, a stairwell) become dramatic moments in the flow of a home.

A mix of materials makes a home's exterior come alive.

Design Fees: You Get What You Pay For

WHEN REQUESTING SUBMISSIONS FOR THIS BOOK, I asked architects to voluntarily reveal their design fees. Most responded. Just like lawyers, architects can provide a wide range of services to address similar problems. In house design, the budget can often only accommodate certain elements of service. In this book, we show projects that have a design fee as a percentage of construction costs ranging from a low of 0 percent (where architects design their own houses) all the way up through 21 percent, where a "full service" of engineering, design, and construction observation was done by the architect.

By describing a wide range of architects' fees and services, this book shows that different architects have different approaches to their work. The reader should understand, however, that inevitably there is a direct relationship between fees paid and services offered. Where fees are at their minimum, the services are at their minimum. The cardinal rule is the less you pay for an architect, the more homeowner time is taken up dealing with the inevitable vagaries, ambiguities, and open questions.

REAL MONEY FOR DREAM HOMES

For homebuyers, cost trumps all other considerations. Housing costs have consistently risen faster than the base rate of inflation, with median prices rising more than tenfold in the last 40 years. Most of us have zero tolerance for fiscal ambiguity when the economic stakes are so high. In an effort to empower the readers of this book, almost all the projects included have their budgets revealed—but read the sidebar (on p. 14) to understand the variables.

Without designs that inspire and reflect the values of housing consumers, there is no need to go through the time and effort required to go beyond stock plans. You cannot spend the same money as you would for a stock spec box and expect to get a custom design of equal or greater size. Your house should fit you—and it can be smaller. It doesn't need all the "bells and whistles" that a developer must put in all his or her models to appeal to enough people to meet a sales quota. Your site is not one of hundreds developed for building, so it will cost more than a spec house plot. But nowhere in

STEEL STAIR. Steel can be either industrial or domesticated, depending on the context. Here, steel railings combined with basic framing lumber produce an expressive sculptural effect. [left]

SMALL MOVES. One subtle gesture—in this case, a curved entry roof—can transform a simple house into a welcoming home. [bottom right, facing page]

your custom-home builder's price can you find the marketing and overhead costs that developers must build into every spec house price tag.

The truth is that if penny pinching were the only reason to write this book, the houses featured would be soulless boxes of stark accommodation. Without the third way of taking control of the choices made in your home's design and construction you could easily declare that "cost is king" and treat your house as an above-ground cave—and many people do just that.

Building a house is not the same as buying a house—the act of construction is unlike any other purchase. There is no base model, because custom homes are derived completely from options. It's the choices that are the heart and soul of the design process.

The Rules: Getting What You Want (and Can Afford)

We view our homes in an inherently paradoxical way. For many of us, a home is our most intimate possession, yet it offers the least opportunity for control even though it's our biggest investment and liability. With all of these high-stakes aspects, the vast majority of Americans in existing housing stock are left with the sad reality that they live in houses of someone else's design, homes that only haphazardly reflect their values and the way they live.

With this attitude, the same consumers who wouldn't choose an automobile because it isn't available in the right color will accept a house that costs ten times as much as that car simply

IN THE LANDSCAPE. The natural world and architecture have always been combined, but the house has a unique place in the landscape. Here, stark buildings serve as a perfect foil to the lush surroundings. [below]

OUTDOOR LIVING. In temperate climates (in this case Mississippi), extending the house into the landscape is not only dramatic and functionally beneficial but it can also evoke a sense of fun. [left, facing page]

BOLD COLOR. Color and wood add life to inexpensive building components, such as low walls and closed-stringer stairs. [middle, facing page]

CREATIVE MATERIALS. Industrial materials can keep the cost of a house down and provide durable and expressive finishes. Here, concrete block and corrugated metal siding surround the courtyard of a house in Texas. [right, facing page]

because it satisfies most of their needs. Our most prized possession has our lowest expectations for personal fulfillment. The simple reason for this misfit is cost. Clearly, if money were no object, every home in America would match its owners perfectly. Cost is the single most important factor for the vast majority of people looking to purchase a place to live.

It's easy to express frustration at the way things are, but how can you actually build well on a budget? This book shows how a number of homeowners have made the choices that allow them to build what they want for the money they have. There are ways to do it. Following are the basic approaches. While not everyone follows all these methods to get the home they

want, every project in this book uses at least some of these guidelines.

1. Use Standard Materials Creatively

Clearly, using mass-produced materials in generic ways saves money over using esoteric products that require artful installation. The dominant technology used in home building in America—dimensional lumber and the sheet-stock system of plywood and drywall—affords real opportunities for containing costs. However, if you let this system be a straitjacket, it can make your home as soulless as the standard spec house. Blandness results unless you reinvent the way you use standard products—and reinvention can be as simple as painting walls in bold colors. If you save money by using standard materials and techniques, you can afford personalized expression elsewhere. Taking stock building parts (such as windows) and arranging them in creative and evocative ways can make the standard special.

2. Shrink to Fit

If you can design your home to fit the way you live while providing for future changes in use, your house can shrink to fit. The tradition in house design in America has been to make homes bigger and bigger so that any number of different lifestyles can be accommodated by the house. The only way to compensate for a lack of "fit" in our homes has been to keep expanding them to accommodate the widest number of potential homebuyers. The average home size in America has more than doubled in the last generation, while family size has shrunk by more than 20 percent in the same time. It would seem that there's some room to spare in the average home.

While logically it would appear easy to pare back size and increase quality, this hasn't happened because families are changing. There are about half the two-parent households there were 30 years ago, and telecommuting, empty-nesting, and an aging population have made many house assumptions obsolete. For example, when one of the families featured in this book realized that their house would have to accommodate children leaving and parents returning, they found no stock plan to fit their lifestyle. So they tailored a 3,600-sq.-ft. five-bedroom home to fit their needs, custom built for the same cost as a stock plan equivalent that would have been 50 percent bigger.

Unless you design in a sense of openness and build in usefulness, you may end up in a house that feels too small. This book shows that you can overcome the feeling of being "squeezed" into too tight a space by artfully aligning spaces and hallways, by providing some spaces that have higher than expected ceiling heights and larger than "normal" window areas, and by directly connecting the inside of your home to outdoor "rooms." The houses in this book show that homes can be smaller than their spec house equivalents without sacrificing beauty to budget.

3. Don't Fight the Site The average lot size has shrunk by 30 percent in the last 25 years, and the buildable sites left around major urban centers are tougher to deal with in terms of slopes, subsoil conditions, and regulations as land around cities becomes scarcer and scarcer. But you can adapt your design to minimize these impacts, as one couple so artfully display

in their sinuously accommodative home in Connecticut.

You may need to change your house plan to adapt to your site. Creating raised terraces or decks on a site that falls off to one side can be unnecessarily costly. If the home can be oriented to have exterior spaces walk out to existing grade, a sloped site can allow a basement foundation to do double duty, both to support the floors above and to enclose naturally lit finished space below.

4. Take Your Time In designing and building custom homes time is money. There is a direct relationship between spending time and spending cold hard cash. The more time you spend figuring out exactly how your house will be used (so that it can "shrink to fit") and the more time spent in "value analysis," the less money ends up being spent. "Value analysis" is a catchall term to describe maximizing the bang for the buck spent for the materials and systems

● ● ● **DESIGNED TO FIT.** Houses should be more than just an assembly of rooms. This home in Washington State, built around a courtyard, combines several distinct occupancies (parents, children, and grandparent) in the spiritual core of the house, its open center.

Being consistent in design doesn't mean being predictable.

BREAKING OUT OF THE BOX. A single curve—in this case, a wall behind the fireplace—can transform the entire ambience of a room and a home. [top left]

OPENINGS AT HOME. One oddball diagonal window (upper left), the openings between stair treads, and the oversized wall of glass at the top of the stair make the interior of this house come alive in a wash of space and light. [top right]

STAIRWAY DRAMA. Steel, wood, drywall, and light create a dramatic vertical space that doesn't cost any more to build than its more generic counterparts.

The Cost of Houses: An Open Book

IN ATTEMPTING TO WRITE A BOOK that focuses on custom-built, one-off houses that are cost competitive to their mass-produced counterparts, it was necessary to put numbers on built designs. There are two inherent difficulties with this: the date of construction and the location of the project. As with all things, houses that were built more than a few years ago have a cost associated with them that is artificially low, and houses that are built in more rural areas reflect a lower cost of construction.

The cost of building the house has been separated from the cost of site development as no two sites are alike. Readers should be able to evaluate these houses as site neutral when trying to figure out how the cost of any particular project relates to their own needs. (In fact, land costs vary so greatly from region to region that their inclusion would confuse more than enlighten, so they are not part of this book.) As with all things, you get what you pay for, and typically the homes with higher budgets have more features, better materials, and more space to deal with similar occupancies.

That being said, with one project's budget not available for publication, the costs of construction for the houses in this book range from a low of $140,000 to a high of $643,000. The projects were built between the mid-1990s and 2002 on sites ranging from densely populated areas to truly rural locations.

used in building your house. You may not need air conditioning for your entire home, but you may need it for the upstairs bedrooms. You may not be able to afford wide-plank maple floors in your home, but you may be able to afford 2¼-in.-wide strip oak flooring.

If time is spent fine-tuning a design and shopping for the right materials at the right price, the window for making mistakes in judgment is dramatically reduced. Conversely, haste does make waste, and the quicker you dive into building your home, the bigger, less efficient, and more expensive it becomes. Just as the classic "one size fits all" spec house expands to prevent misfits, even the best architect and most conscientious owner may have to expand a house when there's not enough time to thoughtfully review its plan.

5. Defer and Save: Building in Phases

When the budget isn't big enough for the "big picture," sometimes a half-a-loaf philosophy allows you to build at least part of the home you

BUDGET BEATER. Using generic materials in unexpected ways (in this case, plywood on the ceiling) can change our perception of a home. When combined with color (the canvas rail at the center) and a "kink" here or there (either in walls that angle or light fixtures that march along the walls), the manipulation of a home's basic parts can beat budgets and surpass expectations.

PHASE ONE, PHASE TWO. The garage (left) was built a couple of years after the main house. It was included in the initial planning, which meant that it became a perfect complement to the house rather than an unexpected interruption. [bottom right, facing page]

want now and allow for expansion in the future. In one Washington State house featured in this book, the architect carefully located walls, windows, and plumbing to allow a finished basement to be slipped in a few years down the road at minimum cost. Attitude is critical in being able to defer what's desirable, but the compelling reality of determining your own home (versus choosing between the lesser of many uninspiring boxes) is often well worth the wait.

6. Take Charge: Spending Time to Save Money

You can save money if you opt to act as your own general contractor. Serving in this role does save money, but you must take on the burden of a large time dump. There may be a 15 percent total savings over a house that has a professional general contractor, but the myriad responsibilities of insurance, scheduling, and management can be a daunting challenge for the average homeowner. Yet for many people the savings in total cost is the difference between having enough money to build a house and having a heartfelt desire and lifelong dream go unbuilt.

Taking the time to personalize your home need not blow your budget. The homes in this book show that there are creative architects and builders who use inspired design and common sense to build affordable homes that reflect the essence of their occupants. You don't need to settle for what's readily available, and you don't have to put your life on hold and quit your job to build your dream. If the house you love in a glossy magazine is out of reach, and if you are left cold by the center-hall colonials marching down a subdivision street, the third way, your way, is shown in the 19 stories of homemaking that follow.

CORNER ATTRACTION. Wraparound steps, a recessed entry, and a multi-tiered shape work with a variety of inexpensive exterior materials to create a welcome combination of shape and shadow.

Stacking Up

WHEN CHARLES G. MUELLER, AN ARCHITECT WITH CENTERBROOK ARCHITECTS, and his wife Tracye realized that the budget to build their dream home had to fall at or under $200,000, they were well aware that they had limits aplenty. The rocky subsoil on their 2½-acre building lot in rural Connecticut would require $20,000 for a septic system, leaving just $180,000 for construction in the pricey New England market. Only resourceful thinking could make those tight funds stretch their value—in this case literally pushing the envelope of the house.

Free architectural design services couldn't change the fact that they needed four bedrooms and at least two-and-a-half baths for their growing family. As for all housing consumers, the Muellers' personal needs had to be addressed or it didn't make sense to build a custom home, so economical materials became the first line of budgetary defense.

LIVING IN A MATERIAL WORLD

The house uses a host of materials usually reserved for commercial buildings, including synthetic stucco and vinyl siding (see the side-

bar on the facing page. Aside from the cost savings afforded by inexpensive commercial-grade materials, another benefit of using so many mass-produced products is that the house was built with miraculous speed—just 5½ months from signing the construction contract to moving in.

Beyond the surfacing products used, costs were contained and time was saved by the use of precut 2x4 studs. The TJI® truss joists used for floors and roof framing span longer distances than their dimensional lumber counterparts, requiring fewer interior supports within the house and making alignments of walls between floors relatively unimportant. Stock windows are used throughout with simple custom muntin patterns. The heating system is as generic as you can get—hot-water-fed baseboard.

FOUR FLOORED

After judicious material selection, the second great economy is making full use of the three floors of the house and the small basement. Mueller was able to squeeze these four levels under the town zoning code's 30-ft. height limit (in this case set from the first floor up) by precise use of the "attic" spaces plus the basement.

The stepped wedding cake layout is inherently efficient, with the widest floor at its base for all the social spaces, a middling

MATERIAL CHOICE

Commercial Grade

IT'S A CLICHÉ TO TELL someone who wants to build a custom home on a limited budget to use stock materials. But almost every aspect of this house uses standard materials in ways that make sense while belying their commercial origins.

Synthetic stucco is seamlessly applied over a cement backerboard to provide a low-maintenance, high-durability finish. Vinyl faux-shingle panels, so often seen in tract housing, find a sense of familiar charm when framed by precisely applied trim (and are easier on the eye the higher they are placed). Split-faced faux stone concrete block, a material that's more at home on shopping malls, here appears to have the muted solidity of a classic early-20th-century bungalow foundation. Plywood with a paintable veneer provides clean surfacing for the prominent eave undersides. The one area of the façade where more costly materials are used to make a statement is the solid wood trim surrounding all windows, facing all eaves, and at the entrance steps.

●●● **LIVING-ROOM THRESHOLD.** In a first floor with few partitions, the living room opens out from the kitchen and extends to the front of the house.

Stacking floors over a small foundation is an efficient use of a house's structure.

A Stairwell to a Heavenly Retreat

IN A HOUSE OF ONLY 2,000 SQ. FT., it's unusual that so much space is given over to a stairwell. Although arguably "inefficient," the stair at the Mueller house has far more functions than simply providing vertical access. First, its 5-ft.-wide base is a small-scale "room," creating a visual event as you walk into the house that belies its true size. The turned bowls set at the newel posts are a humanistic touch that might have been forgotten in the ongoing mind-set of cost containment.

The upstairs hallway, a full 6 ft. wide at the staircase, provides a feeling of openness and play, all bathed in the glow of three windows on two walls. Additionally, Mueller opted to add one step more than the code minimum to each run of the stairs, making the ascent perceptibly gentler than the stock version. It's surprising how a step of less than 7½ in. in height feels so much kinder and gentler than one that approaches 8 in., but it does.

The crowning achievement of this stair is the full three-story vertical space created by its U-shaped layout, which interconnects all three finished levels of this house and provides the one multistory spatial connection between floors.

● ● ● **THE ORGANIZER.** This column-cornered built-in provides structural support at the center of the first floor but also serves as the fulcrum for a pinwheel of trim that spawns soffits and dropped beams, effectively organizing all the spaces of this open plan.

layer for children's bedrooms and a laundry, and the master bedroom suite formed by two rooftop shed dormers at the apex of the house. This is all done with a relatively tiny footprint, minimizing foundation costs. The two sets of shed dormers create a wide variety of under-eave storage, and with such tall gable faces, there is ample opportunity for natural light to penetrate into this efficient little house.

On the face of it, a three-and-a-half-story house of stacked levels made with generic, often commercial-grade materials might sound pretty unappealing, but what makes this house both comforting and visually alive is the careful creativity of a skilled architect. In concert with its aggressive roofscape, the walls of the house use an exposed concrete-block foundation as its base, a faux stucco midriff, and a perfectly triangular gable clad in vinyl shingle panels. This three-part arrangement is saved from predictability by the dramatic windowscaping that dances about all parts, tethered to a horizontal trim band on the first floor but allowed to reign free on the second floor. Only the loftiest third-floor windows respect the natural center line of the roof peak.

LIVING WITHIN THE SHELL

With three stacked floors on a tight footprint, the challenge was to make this 2,000 sq. ft. livable. Charles Mueller pulled this off with several basic moves. First, the common areas of the first floor are all virtually open to each other, centered around a four-column-cornered built-in that pinwheels all parts of the floor about its central presence. This space is also subtly taller than the

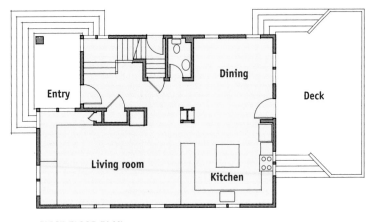

FIRST-FLOOR PLAN

Entry
Dining
Deck
Living room
Kitchen

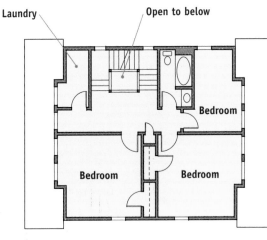

Laundry   Open to below

Bedroom
Bedroom   Bedroom

SECOND-FLOOR PLAN

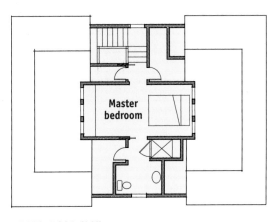

Master bedroom

THIRD-FLOOR PLAN

Location:	Chester, Connecticut
Year Built:	1997
Architect:	Charles G. Mueller, AIA, Centerbrook Architects and Planners
Finished Heated Space:	2,056 sq. ft.
Costs:	Project Budget—$180,000±
	Site Development—$20,000±
	Design Fee—$500 for engineered septic system

FLOOR PLANS

Stacked above each other, the floor plans have clear divisions of use. The first floor contains all the social spaces (inside and out) arranged around a central column. The second floor is given over to three children's bedrooms with a shared bath, while the third level is devoted to a master bedroom suite.

standard 8-ft. ceiling height while still using precut 2x4s, a move that had modest cost in drywall waste but was well worth the small budget bump.

Beyond the open first-floor interior, the broad deck at the back of the house allows for full fair-weather flow from the common areas of the house to the backyard. The other area that breaks the box can be found in the one place that is used by everyone every day. The staircase and adjoining hallways are given enough space, natural light, and handcrafted detail to make their daily encounter a joy. The stair is configured as a "U" shape, which means it has two platforms per level change and three short runs of steps. This configuration allows for a full three-story open shaft of space that connects all floors of the house, a bold gesture given the house's compact design. While there are no two-story spaces in the house, the lofty master bedroom has an arched ceiling as the final spatial reward for the parents.

Interior detailing follows a Shaker sensibility. Flat stock trim, both painted and in natural wood, bands together the window heads. The kitchen cabinets use stock materials in a straightforward way, providing effective storage. Relatively inexpensive veneer plywood is used for the cabinet fronts, while stainless-steel handles and high-tech appliances contrast with the simple millwork. A strategic choice was made in the kitchen to allow a central table for informal dining to expand the already generous counter area.

ENTRY STAIR. The wide stair base serves as an extension of the entry, while the natural wood floors, the corner window, and the careful use of decoration give scale to this comparatively generous space. [above]

NEWEL POST. A stock stair part is transformed into a focal point by the addition of a custom-turned bowl, creating endless possibilities for celebrational decoration. [left]

LIVING ROOM. A continuous band of trim, built-in desks, and doubled windows create a sense of informality amid the rich details.

● ● ● **KITCHEN.** Simple cabinets provide a Shaker-
style backdrop, while a central table
expands the countertop space and presents
a focus for cooking and eating. [above]

BACK SIDE. A broad rear deck extends the
first-floor space into the landscape, while
the stacked dormers break up the expanse
of the large-scale roofscape.

BUILT-INS. Stepped built-ins in the master bedroom, set against a contrasting wall of hand-blocked paint, add a depth of functionality and customization to this tightly designed space. [top]

DINING ROOM CORNER. Wrapping the head trim of these windows around the room and using a different color above and below the trim breaks up the wall's flatness. The trim set in contrast to the dark painted window sash adds a further level of detail. [bottom]

In the Words of ● ● ●
architect Charles G. Mueller

"I feel as though we live in a vacation house. . . . What we like about our house is that it is just what we need it to be, and no more. It's not a big house, but it feels spacious. Its organization is far from formal, but there's a familiar overarching order and breached symmetry that makes it understandable and, as a result, comfortable."

Although having a table set within the work triangle is not a trendy kitchen design, it is one that is tried and true in American culture.

All first-floor spaces have white oak wood floors, a high-durability, high-quality product, while wall-to-wall carpet is a more affordable choice for the bedrooms. Similarly, sheet-vinyl flooring rather than tile is used in the bathrooms to save money. Nothing is cheaper than paint, and color is used to good effect in this house. In the case of the master bedroom, hand-blocked techniques on contrasting walls dress up plain drywall at minimal cost.

SETTING PRIORITIES

With all of this comfortable detailing and architectural expression, some hard choices were made and some opportunities deferred. The 800-sq.-ft. basement has yet to be developed, but it will ultimately house a workout room and informal social areas. The Muellers decided to forego the luxury of a fireplace and deferred the addition of a mudroom. There is no classic master-bedroom walk-in closet, although the space under the eaves provides a fair amount of storage (albeit less than most spec home buyers expect).

All in all, this home has the careful planning, material selection, and meticulous detailing that reflects the optimistic exuberance of homes where necessity is the mother of invention. While it is admittedly easier for architects to apply this level of innovative thinking to their own homes, the wisdom of good choices is clearly evident to anyone wishing to build well on a limited budget.

FACING THE VIEW. The grand sweeping curve of the living room wall is fully apparent from the back of the house, its bold shape complemented by stucco joints, railings, and shading devices. Dense plantings help to obscure the lower level.

Throwing a Curve

AFTER AN EXTENSIVE SEARCH, DENNY BALL AND SHELLEY KERSLAKE REALIZED that there were no homes on the market that were both affordable and met their vision of an expressive contemporary home. Given their frustration, they opted to build their dream house. They found an architect (Brian Brand of Baylis Architects in Bellevue, Washington) who understood their fantasy and who had the skill and experience to create something that is not often found—a unique home in a good neighborhood built within a tight budget. The owners had the good sense to retain their architect prior to choosing a site (whereas most people come to a designer with a lot already in hand). Together, they found a classic south-facing quarter-acre lot on Point Defiance, set among other homes, about 50 miles south of Seattle with spectacular views of Puget Sound. The design of the home was greatly influenced by the site's steep slope, and after zoning setbacks were adhered to, the lot's net buildable area was approximately 50 ft. by 50 ft.

Under the skilled hands of architect Brand, these obvious constraints gave genesis to an open-plan house of clearly expressed shapes and careful detailing. As much as anything else, selection of materials allowed the house to meet its budgetary goals. Dryvit®

HOUSE IN LANDSCAPE. The garage doors are carefully tucked away from view (lower right), while the stark house sits in contrast with the lush plantings.

● ● ● **INSIDE OUT.** The wraparound terrace facing the view becomes a virtual outdoor room that helps extend the interior with large windows and doors.

(faux stucco) exterior surfacing is quite economical when applied in simple, unbroken planes. Virtually every interior surface is covered with drywall, the bottom line in interior cost containment. Details are executed using paint, simple anodized aluminum and painted steel pieces and parts, and stock windows. The home took a full year-and-a-half to design and bid and another year and three months to build. Having ample time to make cost comparisons and research options helped define priorities in ways that a tighter schedule would not have allowed.

SITTING PRETTY

Rather than fight the site, Brand opted to use its southwesterly descent to create a classic "upside-down house" where living areas and master suite are on the upper floor and guest and utility spaces occupy the view-restricted lower floor. This arrangement allowed for a natural split between formal and informal entries, where cars are set below and out of sight and the front door is accessed across a raised terrace that forms the entry threshold to the house. What helps the home feel larger than its 2,700 sq. ft. is that the area given over to the hallway and stair is limited to 240 sq. ft., less than 10 percent of the home's area, which is about half of what's often found in traditional house layouts.

The architect detailed the open and public spaces to fully manifest their potential for drama. The end of the large living

THE VIEW. With the upper level dedicated to living spaces, this is truly an upside-down house. The benefit of this organization is that it affords great views from the common areas. [below]

STOCK FIREPLACE. A standard prefabricated firebox clad in anodized aluminum sheet stock with stainless-steel fasteners makes an interior focal point when the sun goes down. [top left]

ENTRY. Concrete steps and pavers lead to the front door, where a curved rooflet overhead gives a quiet foretaste of the sweeping curve inside.

Saving Money with Curves

HOW DO YOU MAKE CURVED SURFACES LESS EXPENSIVE? The first golden rule is to use true radii (rather than free-line curves). The second is to specify and detail the materials used so that there are no highlighted joints where the curve meets another surface.

In this house, a curved wall joins a curved ceiling, which could have been astronomically expensive if special trim had been custom-fabricated to follow this joint. It would have been more expensive if the wall or roof had paneling or even if different colors of paint had to follow this double-curved interface. In this house, the curve-to-curve relationship is in its most simple and easy-to-execute form. With a drywall-to-drywall inside corner painted all in white, there is no need for craftsmanship or expensive materials to highlight the joint.

● ● ●**SKYLIGHTS AND STAIRS.** Railings spaced between tapered piers bathed in the natural light of skylights above provide a dramatic context for a very simple maple stair. In-floor lights illuminate the piers from below.

area that's set away from the view is focused on the grand internal gesture of a staircase-cum-lightwell. As open vertically as the living area is horizontally, this central spine of space serves to separate the social areas from the master bedroom suite and the entry. A series of skylights, steel rails, and tapering drywall-clad piers ascend into the double-height space. This top-lit volume offsets the potential glare of the south wall of glass.

The stair itself is of clear maple, and it jauntily ramps down to the lower level. Square lights are set into the maple floor and shine up onto the tapered piers and down to illuminate the lower floor. The square motif is echoed throughout the house in the form of large 1-ft. by 1-ft. glass blocks set into the exterior living room wall and large-scale glazing areas in bathrooms and hallways.

Within this architecturally active dwelling, the owner's passion for cooking takes center stage. Because of this priority, the kitchen had to be in full view of all social spaces and also share part of the view that made the site so special. The kitchen design rises to the occasion, sitting at one corner of the ever-widening dining/living room and facing the broad deck that launches forth from the upper floor.

CURVES WITH A CONSCIENCE

There's one other design choice that truly reflects the spirit that drove the owners to build rather than buy the home of their

The Sequence of Entry

Location:	Tacoma, Washington
Year Built:	1998
Architect:	Brian Brand, Baylis Architects
Finished Heated Space:	2,715 sq. ft.
Costs:	Project Budget—$300,000
	Site Development—$45,000
	Design Fee—$45,500

SITE AND FIRST-FLOOR PLAN

The area of the house's footprint is closely defined by the setbacks of this classic quarter-acre suburban lot. The sequence of entry leads through to the vaulted living space, while the central stair serves to separate the master bedroom suite from the rest of the house.

WHEN A HOUSE SITS ON A STEEP HILLSIDE, it's a good idea to make absolutely clear where the front door is amid all the ups and downs. A great deal of effort (and some cost) was put into making the front door of this house a special event.

First, retaining walls were constructed on the downhill side and at the street to build a bridge of retained earth and extend the house to the street. At the threshold of this newly leveled terrace, two cascading concrete steps were formed to face the sidewalk, and these were in turn framed by two carefully cast concrete piers that support a custom gate. This visual bridge is created with large concrete pavers that lead up to the front-door threshold set within a recessed corner of the house. A curved entry rooflet covered by arcing fiberglass panels supported by more concrete piers is the focal point of the approach to the house. These elements combine to make a beginning, middle, and end to the experience of entering a house that lives up to its dynamic interior.

Once you open the front door, an entirely different world of wood, paint, and glass follows through on all the buildup, but for this brief 40-ft. entry path, anticipation is elevated, appreciation is enhanced, and excitement is encouraged at the point of first impression.

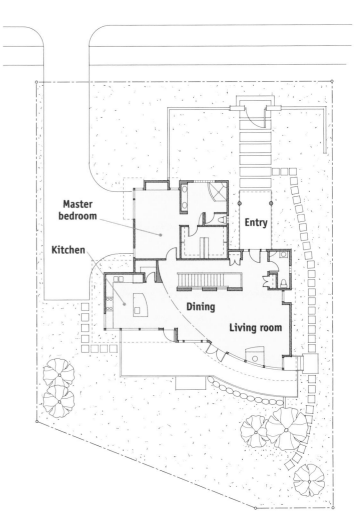

Master bedroom

Kitchen

Entry

Dining

Living room

dreams. The architect chose to take one quarter-radius curve and make it the focal point of the home, not only tying the whole house together but making an unforgettable visual signature from inside and out. With the radius line set to the living room's end wall, the curve organizes the major glazing out to the view and defines the extent of a lightly bowed ceiling over the living/dining areas. This curved wall is made even more dramatic by the careful rhythms of glass-block detailing and window patterning. Reinforcing the dynamic curve is the painted steel lattice sunscreen above the windows and the arcing line of the metal railings that allow the view to be seen while maintaining physical protection. Set in this dramatic swirl of glass, stucco, and metal are the public spaces of the home—living and dining areas and the projecting wraparound terrace that extends the perceived living space.

Curves are typically budget busters in houses built with a specific cost in mind. What makes this curve affordable is that the elements used to make it are stock. The vaulting roof over the living area is made from standard-engineered wood joists hung from laminated wood beams that are glued up to the curve prior to being installed. Where the line of the curved wall intersects these beams, the beams are cut to the line and supported by it, so

MASTER BEDROOM. The scale of the window openings gives this room a dramatic presence, while the sheltering niche for the head of the bed provides a more human scale.

MASTER BATH. Glass block creates a grid, echoing other parts of the house, and provides a great deal of ambient light without sacrificing privacy.

● ●● **THE KITCHEN.** Cabinets and windows wrap around the perimeter of the room, surrounding an elegantly simple kitchen island. Stainless steel, wood, and a view combine to create a feeling of repose.

ompromised.

REPEATED SQUARES. Inserted glass block enriches the double-height living space, providing a contrast to the continuous line of windows below. These small-scale square elements have their shape echoed in the through-floor lights at the stair columns. [top]

EXTERIOR DETAILING. Steel components (all stock with customized fittings) make for an invigorating dance in and about the stucco-clad exterior. [bottom]

the wall and ceiling have a simple compound joint where their curves meet. Since it's a joint between drywall and drywall, with no need for multiply mitered, curved, bent, or crafted trim, it involves no tight tolerances or difficult joints.

With the exception of this one curve, the rest of the house's budget benefits from a straightforward rectangular plan. The only other extravagance is the aforementioned detailing involving metal elements, including lattice, gate, walls, and screens, all supported by cylindrical columns formed by standard concrete pillars. The noncurved portion of the roof is a commercial-grade, surfaced, low-pitch affair with simple internal draining. The arcing roofscape is executed with a standing-seam aluminum roof product (much cheaper than its copper or steel counterpart) that can easily adapt to the consistent curve.

In this home, a gentle curve becomes a focal act in a calm context. If there was more visual competition, the net effect of this one dynamic gesture would have far less impact. The house itself has had a similar impact on the owners' lives, creating a welcome sanctuary for two busy professionals. Here, even a lawyer and a judge can find respite from daily confrontation in the embrace of a home that follows their hearts' desires.

MAIN ROOM. The dining area is set at the narrowed end of the living space formed by an angled wall. The back-side bay window, clear wood floors, window trim, and sashes create a quiet Craftsman-style interior, while the south-facing porch expands the space.

Craftily Done

SOMETIMES THE BEST WAY (OR EVEN THE ONLY WAY) TO BUILD AN AFFORDABLE house is to pick your spots. In this case, a couple in Washington State had found a spot of land that saved money, a heavily sloped quarter-acre lot in a convenient location. The lot had no street frontage, you had to use an easement to get your car within the property's boundaries, and the site dropped about 17 ft. across its 93-ft. length, leaving little room for a stock plan to work. With all these limitations, the land was priced to sell.

In the hands of a skilled designer, a steep slope can afford some benefits. As long as the house parallels the natural contours (rather than being set at an angle to them), it allows for an easy walk out to the lower level and provides light and air to what's normally buried.

The owners were able find just such a skilled architect, one who is used to working with small houses on limited budgets. Ross Chapin's work reflects the spirit of invigorated detailing and material expression that some architects might call traditional, but in truth effectively translates trim, materials, and detailing into the sort of craftsmanship that rewards the eye and the hand upon close encounter. This is comfort architecture that accommodates a lively adaptation of familiar forms to the lifestyles of 21st-century families.

A single detail can enrich an entire house.

LOWER FLOOR. Awaiting interior walls to create separate rooms in a planned future phase of construction, this basement space has fully finished perimeter walls and ceiling. The concrete floors will be surfaced once subdividing walls are installed.

Location:	**Port Townsend, Washington**
Year Built:	2001
Architect:	Ross Chapin
Finished Heated Space:	1,490 sq. ft. (fully finished)
	692 sq. ft. (partially finished)
Costs:	Project Budget—$216,584
	Site Development—$28,000
	Design Fee—$12,000

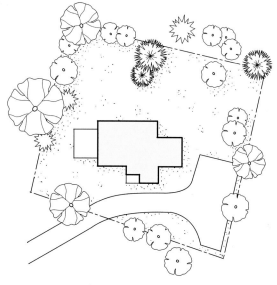

SITE PLAN

Having bought a leftover lot, the owners had to extend the street and its utilities. The benefits were obvious given the wonderful sloping quality of the site.

THE MASTER PLAN

Site improvements ate up $28,000 of the budget (primarily the cost of extending the driveway to the street and hooking up utilities), so the owners had to come up with a strategy that allowed them to build what they could afford now, while designing a house that could seamlessly adapt to their future needs. This can only be done with master planning.

First, the owners and Chapin determined that the interior of the lower level that walked out to grade could be finished later. It would be easy to finish the exterior walls and subdivide this open space into two separate rooms (guest bedroom and studio) at some point in the future as none of the partitions employed would be load bearing. Future sinks and a bathroom had all their plumbing roughed in below the basement slab to allow for easy retrofit. Additionally, on the main level, one end of the house had a window set to accommodate future access for an addition (either a garage or family room). Finally, the house was sited to provide enough room for this future expansion shy of the mandatory setbacks.

SIMPLICITY AND SURPRISE

The plan of the house couldn't be much simpler. The house is organized around a center bearing wall, with a narrow bay on the entry/uphill side and a wider, more open bay facing the view. A small deck extends off the kitchen and dining area, affordably

DETAILS, DETAILS. Open rafter tails and a decorative support bracket frame this classic composition of highly crafted door and light fixture. The carefully cut white cedar shingle siding and colorful trim complete the picture. [left and below]

ENTRY ELEVATION. With no clue that there is a steep slope in the rear, this modest house has the cape-like quality of a single dominant gable roof with a shed roof popping out the top. The roof at the entry extends down and then tilts up in a welcoming gesture.

Beautiful Bays

SIMPLE, STRAIGHTFORWARD DETAILING creates memorable bays out of stock windows. The side walls of these windows are set tight to a few layers of 2x6s picture-framed over the opening so the bay projects out inches, not feet, and there is no cantilevering involved. Rather than the classic sit-in bay window, these windows utilize full trim to create a single large opening in the wall framing the view to the backyard.

The bays use large cottage-style windows, with a smaller upper sash and a larger lower sash. This arrangement solves the dilemma of having the classic double-hung window sash joint (between the upper and lower sashes) set directly in front of your eyes as you are attempting to look out. (It is also a cost-saving feature over having transom windows set over casement units.)

LIVING ROOM/STAIRS. The trimless openings in and around the stairs are formed with prefabricated round drywall corner bead, in contrast to the trimmed-out openings elsewhere. The room is awash in the bathing glow of light from the large bay windows, which brings out the best of the happy ensemble of materials. [top, facing page]

STAIRWAY. A meandering stair uses oversized newel posts to stake out its turf. The beam above is yet another craftsmanly gesture. [below]

The smallest parts of a home often create the greatest delights.

expanding the living space outdoors (critical space when the ground plane slips away dramatically). The interior employs natural materials with charm and subtlety. Kitchen and bath cabinets and stairs are made from carefully crafted oak. The windows throughout have clear-finished pine frames and sashes, which provide a nice contrast with the painted flat stock that surrounds them. With the different thicknesses and projections of trim pieces, all the openings appear to be surrounded by a hand-hewn halo.

It's in the ceiling heights that this 22-ft.-wide by 42-ft.-long house gives its greatest sense of surprise. With such a small perimeter and an unexpectedly low roof at the entry, it's a real treat to walk through the front door and be greeted by a 9-ft. ceiling height. Similarly, although the low perimeter walls of the upper level have the 6-ft. 3-in. minimum wall height, the center (and gable-ended portion) of the roof rises to a full 8 ft. 9 in., as does the entire lower walk-out level, taking full advantage of the steeply sloping hillside.

The second floor neatly fits under the roof form, taking advantage of trusses to minimize the need for internal support. The shape of a house is a critical part of any home's image—especially one sitting on a slope—so the roofscape was a critical feature in Chapin's design. Rather than create a static or predictable roof, he opted to make a single dominant roof form that

● ● ● **SECOND-FLOOR STAIR.** Three small windows at the top of the stairs allow natural light to cascade down to the lower level.

Never underestimate the power of a roof to provide comfort.

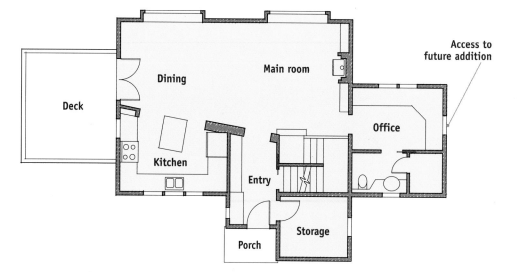

FIRST-FLOOR PLAN

A 22-ft. by 30-ft. central box has a deck to the south, an office and three-quarter bath to the north, and an entry/storage area to the east. The angled wall at the kitchen creates an implied dining space to the left as the main room narrows.

SECOND-FLOOR PLAN

With a tight floor plan utilizing two shed dormers for headroom, the stair weaves up and accesses a tiny hall between master bedroom suite to the left and the guest bedroom to the right. Closets provide maximum sound separation, and the bathroom is economically located directly above the kitchen (combining their plumbing).

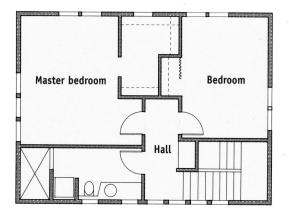

at one point reaches down to within 5 ft. of grade. This low roof extension has a portion peeled up in a lilting curve that compellingly draws attention to a focal point of any home's front façade—the entry. The roof then steps up, accepts a dormer, and uses trim and paint to highlight its animated shape.

To contain costs, the house needed to be smaller than standard size. When fully fleshed out, this home will have three bedrooms, a studio, an office, and two-and-a-half baths, all comfortably stacked in a 2,100-sq.-ft. total building envelope. By having three stories of compact mass, the amount of foundation employed per square foot of space is extraordinarily efficient. Size matters: Less square feet, even when filled with some careful craftsmanship, costs less than anything significantly larger (except for the most generic spec builder's box).

THE BIG IMPACT OF SMALL THINGS

A small, plain house would not have been worth building, and it was Chapin's job to make the final outcome worth all the time and money that inevitably follows a homeowner's dreams. All the careful design decisions could easily have soaked up a fair amount of money given that this house is clad with clear white cedar shingle siding (quite distinct in the land where red cedar shingles rule), a solid oak clear-finished front door, as well as natural wood floors, granite countertops, and eaves with expressively open rafter tails. It is in its lively exterior detailing

DECK. On a sloping site, adding a deck is often the best way to get an outdoor room on the same level as the living space. This simple deck uses the shed overhang to provide shelter for the doors. [top and above]

ROOF FLIP. The tilting uplift of the entry roof has a powerful impact given the straight lines seen everywhere else. This curved roof has its counterpart in the custom-crafted bracket that supports it.

Brackets with a Curve

THE BRACKETS THAT SUPPORT THE ENTRY ROOF and the rooflet leading out to the deck might have been prohibitively expensive if made with built-up/laminated solid wood components. Instead, relatively small pieces of "microlams" (large plywood beams) were used. Because microlams are a structural plywood product these are remarkably stable and exceptionally strong struts, and since they are completely covered by the roofs above the possibility for delamination is minimized.

The builder was given a full-sized template, and the architect created a simple way of attaching the bracket to the wall (using a trim piece that allows the bracket to mount directly to the wall rather than having to deal with the shingle profiles). In this way, a potentially problematic detail was made a good deal easier.

that a potentially plain shape comes close to whimsy. Brackets are sinuously curved (see the sidebar above), and all exterior trim is painted a serene deep blue that perfectly complements the siding. The twin bay windows (see the sidebar on p. 40) have extended eaves and vertical trim lines that surprise and delight, and the rooflet set over the doors going out to the deck has an almost Asian quality of simplified expression.

While clearly these spots were singled out for special treatment, a few other areas of the house had to be left on the proverbial cutting room floor in the interest of meeting the budget. The gable ends were to have had a marvelous trimmed-out apex detail that has been left for a future round of inspired construction, built-ins and a gas fireplace were deferred, and the addition awaits further funding. Custom muntin patterns originally designed for the windows were eliminated as well.

Building your own home reflects many of life's lessons, but more than most projects in this book, this home speaks to a central thesis for anyone's life—namely, making good choices and sticking with them. This may be the only way to get what you want in a situation where limits could easily depress or defeat those who are forced to choose between competing heartfelt desires. The word prioritize does not do justice to this process. It truly tests your mettle when you winnow out those parts of a home that prove to be only desirable (versus essential). The clearer your head and heart, the smaller the window for regret becomes—so small, in this case, that one doubts there are any regrets at all.

KITCHEN. Granite tile countertops (which were installed by the owners) help turn this Shakeresque kitchen into an updated, full-functioning place to eat, cook, and socialize. [top, facing page]

MASTER BATH. A run of small windows across the width of the wall unifies a subdivided space. [bottom, facing page]

BUILT TO FIT. Windows and headboard are carefully sized to fit the joint between the shed and gable roofs. Gable-end windows at left allow some spatial relief to a potentially garret-like space. [below]

DYNAMIC DUO. The smaller studio building (right) is a visual counterpoint to the main house (left), the two shapes tenuously connected by the lightest of bridges, constructed of wire and dimensional lumber. This stark duet sits amid a verdant halo of landscape, planted to become a lush bed for their repose.

Doubled Up

WHEN BUILDING YOUR DREAM HOUSE ON A FIXED BUDGET, it's not enough to have heartfelt commitment. As the owners of this house discovered, you need innovation, patience, and above all, the capacity for hard work.

The owners, a professor and an artist, found a beautiful lot in a meadow framed by a stone wall–lined brook and a backdrop of second-growth trees. While the site's aesthetic ambience was compelling, its practical difficulties proved to be somewhat daunting. Access to the site was by way of a bridge that was in great need of repair, and a number of tightly limiting site factors had to be accommodated, including the active brook, a seasonal stream, the trees, and an existing septic field that was to be reused. Additionally, an unsuitable existing house had to be removed.

As with most enterprises where good intentions come up against the real world, the budget held sway over much of what was done. Ultimately, 1,800 sq. ft. of new construction was built, which not only included two bedrooms and two baths but two full studios (an art studio space and a study/office space) dedicated to the owners' professions.

Location:	**Williamstown, Massachusetts**
Year Built:	1998
Architect:	Burr and McCallum Architects
Finished Heated Space:	1,884 sq. ft.
Costs:	Project Budget—$175,000
	Site Development—$30,000
	Design Fee—$11,500

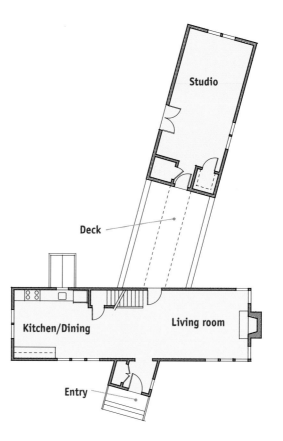

FIRST-FLOOR PLAN

Two prefabricated modular boxes are set at an angle to each other and joined by a simple deck. The line, or *axis*, of the studio box extends through the main building, which is totally open living space, to an angled entry at front.

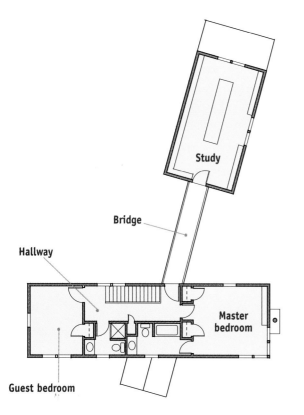

SECOND-FLOOR PLAN

On the second floor, the two boxes are joined by a narrow bridge. In the main body of the house, two bathrooms serve two bedrooms, while a study occupies the upper floor of the studio box.

IN THE LANDSCAPE

The owners understood that their budget was only realistic if they were willing to be open to innovative approaches to construction. Working with architects Andy Burr and Ann McCallum, they opted for a vision of modular housing that defies the preconceived notion that factory-built homes have to be predictable boxes. The architects found the site's "sweet spot" nestled between the existing trees and created two two-story buildings connected by a couple of bare-bones bridges.

The first innovative adaptation of the modular mind-set is the application of the double-high concept (rather than the ubiquitous double-wide layout). In other words, rather than attaching prefabricated boxes side by side, this home is in two separate pieces, with single-wide second-floor modules stacked over first-floor modules. The boxes used to create this home are the standard maximum width (13 ft. 9 in.) and follow a 15-ft. module applied to the lengths of both buildings (30 ft. long for the studio structure and 45 ft. long for the house itself).

ENTRYWAY. The entry portico is the focal point of the long approach to the house from the street and driveway. The steps are formed of some of the least expensive materials available—pressure-treated wood and steel cable, basic materials honestly assembled to reinforce a strong design.

Corrugated Clapboard?

WHEN SEEN FROM A DISTANCE, the simple shapes of the house appear to be sided with gray clapboard with some interesting trim lines. But as you get closer, you realize that the siding is anything but the classic material of so many 19th-century farmhouses. Rather than sided with thin pieces of wood lapped over each other, this house is clad with large sheets of 26-gauge corrugated steel painted with an industrial-strength coating. When its rippling lines are oriented horizontally, you get the look of clapboards, but with an interesting visual vibration that subtly enlivens the simple shapes.

Kynar® paint was applied as a factory finish, the highest-durability coating readily available. While not inexpensive in the short run, the coating is said to outlast anything applied to wood, and since the per-foot cost of painted-wood clapboards and this siding turned out to be equivalent, this product wins the price war on an average yearly cost basis.

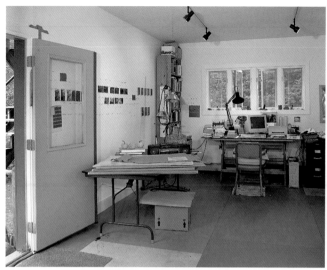

STUDIO SPACE. Painted plywood floors
and clean lines accommodate the
professional world that coexists with the
separate domestic reality beyond.

If these prefab units were simply dropped on the landscape and comfortably clad in predictable materials, the design would probably be livable but hardly unforgettable. The big move of Burr and McCallum was that when they separated the buildings, they also skewed their orientation to each other and extended that skew through the main house to create an angled entry that lines up with the view of the house as seen from the driveway. This light angle, barely perceptible when seen from a distance, becomes surprisingly dynamic when the building is experienced up close.

Similarly, the exterior materials that clad these simple, symmetrically gabled boxes seem relatively predictable when seen from afar. But upon closer inspection, the two-tone diamond-patterned asphalt roofing shingles and the subtly painted corrugated steel siding, when combined with brightly painted yellow exterior doors, make for a deeply satisfying sense that the standard has been lovingly tweaked by the designers (in this case, with the enthusiastic cooperation of the homeowners).

THINKING INSIDE THE BOXES

The interior layout of the house allows some very simple economies. The two upstairs bathrooms are centrally located and built back-to-back, isolating the plumbing. The stair is a straight stock affair with walls on both sides of its run, which is cheaper

In the Words of ●●●

architects Andy Burr and Ann McCallum

"The tight budget prevented us from having the time to execute a full set of construction details and greatly limited the time available for site visits. Phone calls and direct negotiations between the owners and subcontractors bridged the gap between what was designed and what was created in the field."

KITCHEN. Large, double-hung windows with a clerestory plate-glass transom above enliven an otherwise modest eat-in kitchen made with the simplest of cabinets. Industrial light fixtures provide contrast amid the sea of white-painted wall surfaces. [above]

GUEST BEDROOM. Oversized windows in a tight space make for a sense of home and harbor, while the low windowsills allow uninterrupted views from bed. [left]

TOP OF THE STAIR. The windows at the top of the stair direct light down to the middle of the plan below. The railing echoes those used outside, while the wood floors add a gently domesticating touch to this simple space. [right, facing page]

FROM THE SOUTH. With the front entry porch (left) cast at an angle to its parent building, the house is a simple shape upon which a chimney and flue are applied (right), with windows wrapped around its corners or individually set. The studio outbuilding (right) follows through on the angle of the protruding entry, which appears to be shot through the house like an arrow. [above]

STUDIO. Stark and simple as architecture can be, the two screen doors to the studio are beacons of yellow set amongst the sea of prepainted corrugated steel. [left] Access to the second floor is via a bridge-cum-gangplank, whereas the lower access is a full deck. [right]

Tweak the details and surface materials to

The Little Roof That Could

ASPHALT SHINGLES ARE THE COMMON CURRENCY of inexpensive homes in America. "Three-tab" are the simplest and cheapest and usually have the shortest life expectancy. "Architectural" have layers of applied pieces, colors, and faux shadow lines in an attempt to imitate natural materials. However, in this house, a specialized variant of a low-cost product was used: "French Estate" asphalt shingles, simple single-ply asphalt roofing that's "diamondized" or "fish scaled" to create a tantalizing diagonal pattern. Using two colors creates a truly glistening effect. Large copper staples hold the shingles in place, and the visual enrichment is plain to see.

than a stair with an open railing at its side or one with winders, a platform, or curves. Heating is simple hot-water convection baseboard, with separate systems for the house and studio. The flooring in the common areas is standard strip-wood flooring, while other areas have vinyl. The main house has the luxury of a full basement, while the studio is afforded the economy of a crawl space. Access to the second-floor study is totally separate from the studio below, via a bridge set within the wide hallway in the second floor of the main house.

Beyond the material selections that add visual excitement, simpler gestures prevent this home from being awkward or predictable. In the living room and the master bedroom, the outsized double-hung windows wrap around corners, increasing their impact. All the interior spaces are surprisingly open and light-filled because the narrow width of the boxes allows light to be present from three sides. A prefabricated fireplace is tacked onto one end, its projecting flue perfectly aligned with the centerline of the gable. The skewed entry pavilion jauntily pierces the potential billboard flatness of the long dimension of the main house, as do the bridges between the boxes, which are aligned with the entry. A single-story shed extension off the studio building animates its basic shape. Horizontal bandings of trim at the joints between the corrugated sheet-stock siding relate to window-sills, roof peaks, and other architectural features.

make factory-built housing your own.

SECOND-FLOOR THRESHOLD. Yellow paint and clear-finished wood provide contrast to the pervasive use of painted drywall and flat trim inside and industrially coated steel outside. [left]

LIVING ROOM. Double-hung windows are ganged and wrapped around corners to provide visual access to a broad sweep of the landscape, while a standard firebox is highlighted with bold tiling and centered on the gable-end wall to form the nighttime focus for this social space. [right]

It would be natural to expect that modular assembly would translate to savings in construction time. But that wasn't the case here. The owners saw an anticipated 60-day construction period turn into an eight-month marathon during which the emotional rush of modular assembly was tempered by the ongoing customization of the basic boxes into the final inspiring product. For half of this eight-month period, the owners lived in the house and, in their words, "did nothing but paint, sand, and deal with constantly evolving construction problems."

The final result of so much effort was clearly worth it. While a garage had to be deferred (though still planned for), the home functions much larger than the owners anticipated, and the total budget of approximately $200,000 speaks volumes about the human spirit. In the costly New England construction climate of the late 1990s, this shining example of the courage and dedication of the homeowners, combined with the inspiration of the architects, gives hope to everyone who comes in contact with this dynamic duet.

STUDIO. Once inside, the logic behind the saw-toothed exterior becomes obvious, with massive clerestory windows set to each tooth's vertical edge. Much like the rest of the house, the consistent use of industrial products (in this case the windows) makes the house a true hybrid of work and domesticity.

Working Home

CASEY AND JOANN WILLIAMS FIRST HIRED TAFT ARCHITECTS TO DESIGN a home for them in the mid-1980s, at a time when this Texas firm was fresh on the scene of cutting-edge architectural design. That house was the Williams's dream home, and their long-term friendship with architects John J. Casbarian and Danny Samuels of Taft Architects was cemented by the positive experience of collaborating on house number one.

The Williamses both work in visual and craftsmanly fields. Casey is a photographer and a painter, whose work needs large spaces for its full development. Joann is a jewelry artist and art therapist who needs far less space, and more focus than light and air. Their '80s dream house was so focused on the domestic that the outsized storage space needed for Casey's work was accommodated in a warehouse, and their individual studios were in yet another location. The Williamses realized that they needed to change their house to bring the parallel universes of career and home together. "This is a return to the old style," Joann Williams notes, alluding to the apartment-above-the-shop living arrangement that housed so many families over the last few centuries. Because of these combined functions, the architects divined a path that was in stark contrast with their original work for the couple.

CEILING LEVEL. Simple trusses support the roof above and accommodate ductwork below. This lofty ceilingscape spans between the twin two-story wings of the house and serves as a gathering place filled with light, space, and dramatic structure.

LIVING/DINING SPACE. The wood trusses are combined with the carefully laid out lighting, windowscaping, walls, and concrete flooring to create an open space that neither panders to the domestic nor is stridently institutional. [below]

WHEN WORK COMES HOME

The design process remained the same, starting out with multiple options to give the Williamses the chance to see what was possible. But while Casbarian and Samuels came up with seven initial schemes for the first house, only three design alternatives were needed for this second effort. Even though this house had to accommodate far more functional diversity—home and workplaces—the designers and their clients realized that these twin worlds were best housed in a simple, open home. Personalized scale and idiosyncratic detailing is comfortable for our intimate spaces, but working at home demands a little professional distance.

It should be pointed out that this home is in Texas, a land that seldom gets frigidly cold and is thoroughly enmeshed in an agrarian sensibility. The architects used this fair-weather context to help allow workplace and hearth to coexist functionally. Casey's studio has no interior connection to the house, and entry to both home and studio is under cover but outside.

If this were just a stark Modernist box used as a blank slate upon which life is lived and work is done, the house would be more like a warehouse than a home. Casbarian and Samuels knew that the home had to reflect its owners' values as a family as much as it embraced their careers. In their effort to bring

● ● ● **LOOKING OUT FROM THE KITCHEN.** Hidden from the view of the dining room table but fully bathed in the light of the living area's clerestory windows, the kitchen seems freed of its normal domestic grind. Using windows as a backsplash between upper and lower cabinets to the right reinforces the exceptional simplicity and starkness of all the elements.

In urban areas, homes either make their own sites or they are owned by the neighborhood.

On the Grid

MORE THAN ANY OTHER PROJECT IN THIS BOOK, this house follows a right-angle layout grid—expressed by grooves raked into the concrete floor. The basic grid is 8 ft. by 8 ft., which is then broken down further into a 4-ft. grid for virtually every plan element of the house save a few necessary anomalies. Ordering the house's superstructure using this consistent grid pattern not only helped minimize layout time but also reinforced the sense of the project's crisp modern aesthetics.

FIRST-FLOOR PLAN

The two wings of the house frame a courtyard, which is sheltered on the south-facing side by a wall of vegetation.

SECOND-FLOOR PLAN

The street-side wing is a full studio for large-scale artwork, while the backyard-facing second floor is completely given over to master bedroom and study workspace.

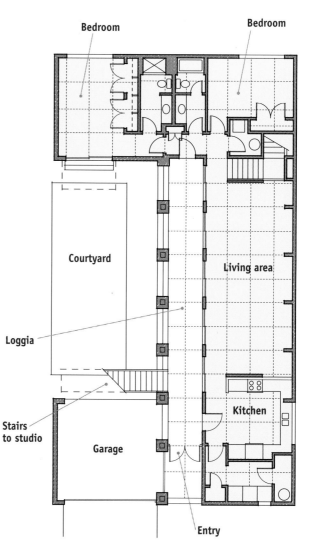

Bedroom

Bedroom

Courtyard

Living area

Loggia

Stairs to studio

Garage

Kitchen

Entry

FIRST-FLOOR PLAN

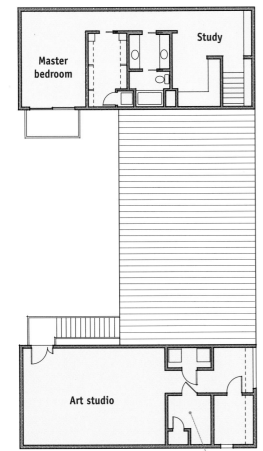

SECOND-FLOOR PLAN

Master bedroom

Study

Art studio

Storage

Location:	**Houston, Texas**
Year Built:	1996
Architect:	John J. Casbarian and Danny Samuels, Partners, Taft Architects
Finished Heated Space:	3,100 sq. ft.
Costs:	Project Budget—$300,000 Site Development—withheld Design Fee—withheld

home to the workplace, the architects infused all pieces and parts with a lightly romanticized use of materials seen in many Texas farms. Galvanized steel, chain-link fence, and concrete are carefully detailed to be humanized, with a level of finish that's anything but industrial.

TIGHT SITE

Located on the type of tight lot prevalent in many subdivisions sprawling around our urban centers, this house is bound by setbacks that create some very snug siting conditions. Rather than try to pretend that this is a typical suburban home with room for swing sets and manicured lawns, the architects realized that in order to have any degree of privacy, the house had to make full use of whatever space was available from this ⅛-acre patch of ground. The house is set tight to the setbacks on a 103-ft. by 53-ft. site and lays out to form a "C" shape in which the short legs of the house face the street on one side and take up all the rest of the available site to the rear. An open common area and loggia spans between these two short wings. The outdoor space created by this 3,100-sq.-ft. house is an urban courtyard whose fourth side is formed by lush foliage that grows rampantly in the semitropical Texas climate.

LIVING ROOM. Standard materials, simply organized, create a sense of calm order and transparency. Steel conduit supports and coordinates light fixtures, while a partial wall (right) obscures the stair beyond. The concrete floor slips seamlessly between inside and outside, blurring the distinction between the two worlds.

MATERIAL CHOICE
Dressing Up the Columns

MOST COLUMNS ARE LITTLE MORE THAN a rude connection between support at the base and what is being held up at the top, but others make art out of necessity. In this house, simple steel columns are dressed up with stock concrete block layered around them. The slender steel column is revealed at a level that aligns with the height of the sliding doors that sit opposite them in the loggia they both define. By combining materials (block, wood, and steel) and geometries (rectilinear and splayed), this recurring element becomes both structure and art within the context of a house whose plan is organized around a tight grid.

●
●
●

FROM THE CORNER. When combined with a sidewall of vegetation (left), the house is organized to form an urban retreat, a courtyard that is held distinct from the hubbub of the city. [facing page]

HIGH-TECH GARAGE. Transparent garage doors (with pulleys, cable, and chain-link fencing set within tubular-steel frames) allow a screened view through to the inner courtyard. All the ground planes are set at the same level (whether poured concrete, pavers, or grass), making the outdoor world feel like part of the built environment. To the right of the garage, a row of columns defines a path along the edge of the courtyard.

● ● ● **COURTYARD.** Basic wood framing supported by equally simple struts and posts bears on oversized pillars formed of generic concrete block, all set to an over-sized height (14 ft.) and thoroughly contained by the sheet metal wings that form the two short ends of the courtyard.

The wing that faces the street has a virtually open two-car garage and entry, as well as kitchen and utility spaces. Casey's studio and storage spaces occupy the second floor of the wing. The rear-facing wing, identically sized at 17 ft. 8 in. by 42 ft., has two guest bedrooms with their own separate bathrooms below and the master suite and Joann's studio on the second floor. Both workspaces have walk-out balconies that face the courtyard. The 40-ft.-long by 16-ft.-wide living space is a full two stories high, using wood trusses and struts above a wall formed with inexpensive sliding glass doors set between piers clad in concrete block. A parallel set of piers runs along the edge of the courtyard.

SOPHISTICATION ON A BUDGET

Because of poor subsoil conditions, the house required a relatively expensive foundation, involving about 40 cast-concrete piers that support a grid of heavily reinforced concrete grade beams. This meant that costs above the foundation were a big issue. The industrial aesthetic of the home's palette of materials (concrete, steel, wood, and white-painted drywall) certainly saved money. Corrugated steel and concrete block are tough, prefinished sheet materials that are easy to install, while the wood elements are stock pine boards. The roofs are all directly supported simple-span affairs with no hips (but with some internally draining valleys).

Industrial materials are instantly domesticated when the detailing respects the intima

● ● ● **STUDIO ACCESS.** An exterior stair provides independent access to the art studio that occupies the street-facing second-floor wing of the house. [top left]

OVERLOOKING THE COURTYARD. A Juliet balcony cantilevered off the master bedroom suite looks into the courtyard. The double-height wing serves to shield the courtyard from unwanted views and the urban din that surrounds it. [above].

MASTER BEDROOM. Set within its own individual roof sawtooth, the master bedroom has a direct extension into the courtyard through oversized sliding-glass doors. The large areas of white painted drywall reflect and diffuse light descending from the huge clerestory roof windows, bathing the wood, concrete, and steel in a brilliant glow. [top right]

DINING/KITCHEN. Carefully screened by a central panel, the simple palette of materials (concrete below, wood and steel above, and drywall all around) makes for a serene yet active space. [facing page]

Mechanical equipment is set in open space or directly on walls—there's no need to hide things with decorative arts when open space is the order of the day.

But the overriding method of cost containment is in the gridded organization of all elements below the roof—the builder's dream method for layout and construction without the need for custom craftsmanship. There's scarcely a curve or angle anywhere in the entire house, except for the angles necessary to create the sawtooth roof and the stair stringers that allow access to the second floor. By being relentlessly rectilinear, Casbarian and Samuels have given their clients the gift of light and openness on a budget.

Clearly, it takes architectural skill to pull off this sense of scale, space, and sophistication using industrial materials and gridded geometry (and it didn't hurt that clients and architects were lifelong friends). This edgy aesthetic may be hard for some to call "residential," but that's why everyone needs to be true to their own muse when thinking about their own house. In this case, not only did the vision perfectly accommodate the split-screen world of life and art, but it also facilitated building a dramatic and accommodating home with an affordable price tag.

THE FRONT. With its strong symmetry, the overarching centerline of a gable roof helps determine the position of the front door. This dramatically simple shape maintains its presence while serving as the context for a variety of window shapes (diamond, bay, gridded, and isolated).

Beauty on a Budget

NANCY AND MICHAEL JOHNSTON FACED A CLASSIC DILEMMA.

They had inherited a house with mixed blessings. The positives were plain to see: The house faced a community green (the site was originally a spiritualist compound formed almost 100 years ago in Niantic, Connecticut), and the back side offered a wonderful panoramic view of the Niantic River framed by mature maple trees.

The one clear downside was the site's microscopic size (approximately ⅛ acre). It's a fact of life that most waterfront homes built before the 1960s are considered "preexisting" or "nonconforming" by current local zoning laws. In other words, what is now in place could not have been built today, so there are special limitations to any new construction that may be built on these sites. In planning a new house, the Johnstons had to build on the existing footprint and carefully rebuild the shed shape on one side to match the original house, which left them virtually no wiggle room.

A SLOW PROCESS

As with many two-income families seeking to create a home, the thought of building a new house was fraught with financial concerns for the Johnstons. They had a budget of $160,000 in 1995. Given the limitation of the existing footprint, the house could only

STOCK DOORS, NICE FINISH. These doors are straight out of the catalog, mass-produced for economy, but they are made with vertical-grain solid-pine panels and coated with clear urethane to give them a visually rewarding appearance. [left]

A CARPENTERLY DETAIL. Set at the joint between the posts and the roof over the master bedroom walk-out porch, this careful combination of stock pieces turns a potentially awkward joint into an interesting design feature. [far left]

grow by building a second story, which would increase the size to between 1,500 sq. ft. and 2,000 sq. ft. The project progressed through sporadic bursts of design activity, regulatory approvals, bidding, and so on during a three-and-a-half-year process of design and permitting and, of course, the unavoidable increase in construction costs over time. Throughout all the ups and downs of the approval process, the owners remained steadfast in their resolve to build the house, and they ended up with a $200,000 price tag for an 1,800-sq.-ft. house that had two-and-a-half bedrooms and one-and-three-quarter baths.

What made containing the budgetary creep even more challenging was the homeowners' desire for high-quality, durable, and aesthetically expressive materials and features. They chose wood siding (not vinyl), wood flooring (not carpet), a wood-burning fireplace (not gas), high ceilings, and some crafty windowscaping using high-quality windows. The final product is a combination of open space and careful detailing built within extraordinary limits, a beacon of hope for average housing consumers who think that they can't afford a custom home.

BIG MOVES IN A SMALL HOUSE

To make the wish list real, a variety of approaches were employed to "ease the squeeze" of a relatively small house set within a fixed footprint. First, visual connections were made through the interior to take advantage of the rewarding waterfront

BACKSIDE PORCH. A simple stoop, built from inexpensive pressure-treated wood, is scaled to form the social edge between house and landscape. This tight community has tiny side yards between houses, so the rear yard needs to be fully accessible.

● ● ● **THE "WALK-IN" VIEW.** Directly opposite the front door, the living room drops down three steps and double doors guide the view out to the water beyond.

MATERIAL CHOICE

The Higher You Go, the Cheaper You Can Get

MATERIALS CAN LOSE THEIR SENSITIVITY to human contact the farther they are removed from view or touch. Just as a billboard that looks quite intricate proves to be clumsily rendered when seen up close, simple stock materials can be used in custom construction to save money—as long as they are removed from direct examination.

The chimney shroud in this house is covered with of one of the least expensive materials available (T1-11 plywood), and the soffit is a prefabricated perforated aluminum material that simulates a tongue-in-groove wood product. This soffit material prevents the need for a separate venting strip and is also far less expensive than the painted wood surface that was used above the entry. Neither chimney nor eave is within close viewing or touching distance, and both standard materials are subtly introduced to save thousands of dollars.

From Stock Windows to Custom Wall

BY GANGING TOGETHER A WALL of stock windows and surrounding them with trim of uniform width, it's possible to make separate parts into a single visual entity. When creating such a large-scale opening in a house, care has to be taken to maintain the stiffness of the exterior walls.

Plywood is the miracle material that allows light, wood-framed homes to have a great deal of stiffness given the thinness of their walls. When making a lattice of dimensional lumber that will accept windows, that stiffness has effectively been compromised as there are no large areas of plywood that can brace the structure. In this house, stock steel angle braces were used at every corner, compensating for the lack of surface area for plywood.

FIRST-FLOOR PLAN

A recessed entry opens onto an intermediate foyer that feeds off to a den/guest bedroom on one side and a stairwell on the other. Steps lead down through the main living space to the double doors beyond.

Location:	Niantic, Connecticut
Year Built:	1999
Architect:	Duo Dickinson
Finished Heated Space:	1,800 sq. ft.
Costs:	Project Budget—$190,000
	Site Development—$15,000
	Design Fee—$12,000

vista. The visual connection starts at the front door, where the view opens up from the raised foyer through the living room and out double doors that are set into a grid of windows facing the river.

Second, the open space of the first floor was used to help overcome the feeling that this is only an 1,800-sq.-ft. house. The refrigerator turns its back to the entry and is fully clad with walls and a "roof," allowing anyone entering the house to see over the refrigerator out to the water view.

SPLURGE HERE, SAVE THERE

A number of custom touches enliven the house: a covered walk-out porch for the master bedroom, a bay window for the son's bedroom, a built-in shroud for the television, and the expressive exterior trim—all wrought of standard parts brought to life by simple coordination of line, color, shape, and material. With the deep blue front door and cool gray clapboards, the white trim becomes a coordinating element that wraps around corners, defines grids, and highlights features. There is one truly luxurious custom piece in the house: the granite countertop set to the raised lip of the island, making the stock cabinets fade in comparison to its sinuous line and lustrous presence.

Structure was simplified to reduce costs. Two framing bays, one on the kitchen side of the house, the other on the living-room side, are supported by a central beam, which in turn is

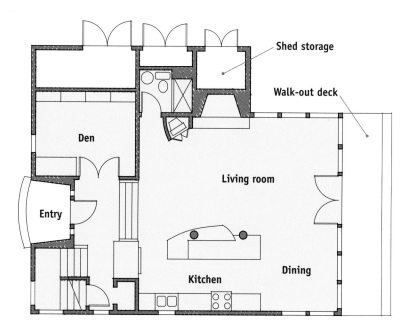

● ● ● **ENTRY/STAIR.** The stair forms a lightwell, with its windows and operable skylight helping to vent the entire house. By boxing in the refrigerator with a drywall shroud, the back of the appliance is out of view from the front door.

LIVING ROOM CORNER LOOKING OUT TO THE WATER.
Wrapping around the corner, a pattern becomes a
transparent shape. Gridded stock parts contrast with
the trees and river to the benefit of both. [above]

THE KITCHEN. The cabinets are stock items, but the
overall impact of the kitchen is elevated by the
custom-crafted island formed by stock columns and
a gently curving granite countertop. The raised
counter provides a barrier between the mess of
cooking and the social side of the home. [top and
bottom right]

In a sea of white paint a single splurge can have a transforming effect on an entire interior.

FROM THE CORNER. The wraparound trim and windows combine with eave lines to tie the facades together, while the projecting bay window and recessed entry create a simple three-dimensional focal point. [left]

DINING ROOM. A corner space tucked behind the kitchen, the dining area is defined by wraparound windows but safely out of view from anyone entering the house. [below]

supported by two columns. The roof is a symmetrical gable tied together by the ceiling of the second floor, which forms the floor of the attic. The roof peak soars to create a large attic, with windows that allow natural light. When combined with a full basement, this small house functions much larger than you might expect.

PEOPLE POWER

It's not just design that keeps cost down, it's also the can-do spirit of the owners. The Johnstons themselves subcontracted out the electrical work and purchased cabinets and bathroom fixtures directly (all stock elements).

Knowing the limits that were present, the architect worked on an hourly basis using some of his lowest-billing dollar-per-hour employees and a sympathetic engineer to keep total design fees down to about 5 percent of the construction cost. Many questions were answered by phone, and e-mailed digital photographs often took the place of the architect's on-site presence and detail drawings. The project was blessed with builders Sutherland and Krause, who had a wealth of common sense and hard-edged integrity and commitment in a situation with little or no budgetary leeway. They were local builders, interested in the community, who went the extra mile to make a tight budget into a beautiful house.

One of the main things that keeps home design fresh and challenging for residential architects is that no two scenarios are ever alike. In this case, an abundance of limits was overcome by the dedication of all parties concerned. "We are very happy with both the design and construction," Nancy says, "and overjoyed that we are able to stay on the water and stay connected with our family heritage."

THE COURTYARD. The sweeping line of the curving wall connects two independent residences at the courtyard. Vertical siding follows the curve with ease, and freestanding columns take the weight of the roof off the wall, freeing the curve of any need to align with its support.

Spiral Solution

TWENTY-FIRST-CENTURY AMERICA IS A TAPESTRY OF EVER-EVOLVING
family types, and an ever-increasing number of nontraditional families on the fringes of this tapestry are being accommodated one house at a time. In this case, a couple with three children, two of whom have left the nest and one of whom will soon do so, decided to build their own home but at the same time accommodate one of their parents, who in turn wanted to be with her sibling. So Paula and Steve Leitz, and at times some or all of their children, together with "the Grams," would all live together as one extended family under a single roof.

For most potential homeowners, the perceived cost of building a custom home simply doesn't allow them to consider it as an option. Given the Leitzes' unique needs, the hard-edged reality was that the available housing stock simply didn't accommodate their new family organization. To build a house for this unique scenario, the Leitzes went to their friend Bret Drager of Drager Gould Architects. They found a classic suburban two-acre site and used a generic palette of materials. It is in the dance of these predictable parts with the idiosyncratic family organization that the architect created a memorable residence for five relatively independent people, with accommodations for two even more independent visitors.

●●● **BUILT-INS.** A wall of built-ins in the great room balances the impact of the curving wall to the right. The floor is rich Brazilian cherry. [above]

EAVE DETAILS. Simple trim and stock windows conspire with inexpensive siding to make a visually active house. [top left]

FRONT FAÇADE. A carefully composed façade has some surprises: a reverse-pitched, light-scooping shed dormer (center), an exposed metal flue, and larger-than-normal overhangs. The curved walkway gives a hint of the spiraling courtyard wall that lies inside. [top right]

MANY PARTS, ONE HOUSE

Drager was able to efficiently accommodate a five-bedroom, four-and-a-half-bath home within a 3,645-sq.-ft. house. In addition to the higher-than-normal bedroom and bathroom count, the house required two separate social spaces for the two basic occupancies (the Leitzes and the Grams). Additionally, a three-car garage was a virtual necessity given the number of occupants. The budget for all of this construction, including site improvements and design fees, was just over $500,000, a price that's competitive with the standardized "undesigned" counterparts in the area. It helped that the fee for architectural design was virtually at wholesale rates given the preexisting relationship between the Leitzes and architect Drager.

Drager effectively created two houses joined on the inside by a common entry and on the outside by a courtyard, which in turn is organized around a sinuous spiral that provides a common focus for all the public spaces. The interior is a four-part harmony: the three-car garage and entry; a master-bedroom-down house complete with its own great room and kitchen; "the Grams' Cottage," comprising a separate kitchenette, common living area, and two extra bedrooms in the form of a suite with its own bathroom; and a fourth component (tucked away upstairs out of

The central spiral gives this house its common identity as a single home for many people.

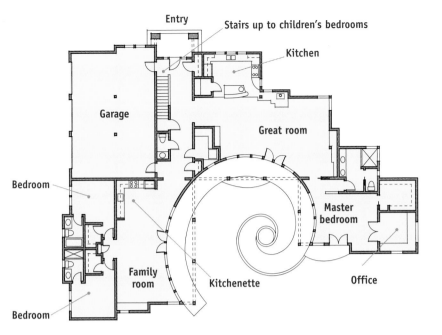

Entry

Stairs up to children's bedrooms

Kitchen

Garage

Great room

Bedroom

Master bedroom

Family room

Kitchenette

Office

Bedroom

FIRST-FLOOR PLAN

The sinuous spiral, which extends into the courtyard, provides the essential connection between the two separate residences ("Grams" to the left and parents to the right). The stairs at the entry lead up to a two-bedroom one-bath apartment for the kids above the garage.

Location:	Gig Harbor, Washington
Year Built:	2002
Architect:	Drager Gould Architects
Finished Heated Space:	3,645 sq. ft.
Costs:	Project Budget—$475,000
	Site Development—$20,000
	Design Fee—$14,700

● ● ● **ALONG THE CURVE.** At the dining area, the curved wall bows into a space that has a vaulted ceiling. The consistency of the trim inside and out coordinates the view from the window out to the rest of the house.

Spiral Roots

THE SPIRAL THAT CREATES THE COURTYARD WALL and the detailing of the central courtyard is based upon the Golden Mean, an architectural organizing system, also known as the Fibonacci Series. This is a proportional system where the ratio of size is ever increasing, and it can readily be seen in the cross-section of the conch shell, in esoteric books on Renaissance architectural theory by Andrea Palladio, and in the work of the French Modern master Le Corbusier.

In a true Fibonacci curve, there is an infinite number of radii employed to create the curve. For the sake of practical construction, architect Drager determined that this spiraling curve could be made from a finite series of radii set to specific points in the line of the curve.

sight and flow) of two visiting children's bedrooms with their own bath set above the garage. All the service spaces are adjacent to or feed off of the common entry, including a half-bath and laundry as well as a tiny full basement below the entry space, which is used for mechanical equipment.

BUILDING THE PARTS

Aside from keeping the square footage under control, Drager managed to contain costs on this project in a number of straightforward ways. First, he used prefabricated roof trusses over three-quarters of the building, which meant that the walls below them could be non-load-bearing. Second, most of the house is built above crawl space rather than a full basement, saving money over full-height column supports and concrete foundation walls.

Beyond the savings afforded by the house's structure, costs were also contained by using inexpensive materials. An asphalt shingle roof and generic vinyl windows along with a universal interior finish of painted drywall and flat stock trim kept the detailing of the house simple. On the exterior, 12-in.-wide knotty cedar boards are used in board-and-batten siding and eave detailing. Using these plain, inexpensive materials has the added benefit of focusing attention on the more elaborate entry and courtyard.

● ● ● **MASTER BEDROOM.** The curved wall terminates at the master bedroom, where deeply extended eaves afford protection from sun and rain over the French doors. Inside, clerestory windows in the vaulted ceiling bathe the space with natural light. [right and facing page]

Use expressive materials where they do the most good, both functionally and visually.

In addition to using standard techniques and generic materials, Drager employed some subtle "value analysis" to reduce costs. Running a ¼-in. tongue-and-groove plywood subfloor below the floor finishes allows tile floors to coexist with wood floors in the same plane without the problems of adding concrete or more plywood under the tile. The laundry and three of the four-and-a-half bathrooms have inexpensive vinyl flooring, and stock 1-ft.-square ceramic tile is used for both kitchen and entry halls, with stone tile for countertops rather than its more expensive slab counterpart. Kitchen cabinets were kept simple as well. The stairs going up to the second-floor children's bedrooms are closed-stringer construction (which is cheaper than the open zigzag of exposed treads and risers), with stock newels, balusters, and handrails. Although the interior trim is all flat stock, the material is clear hemlock, and the doors, while stock, are of a grade of wood that allowed for clear finish as well.

SPICING IT UP

While most of the materials and detailing of the house are generic, architectural spice is added through the selective application of relatively expensive materials at places of maximum exposure—for example, the highly visible Brazilian cherry flooring in the great room, the fieldstone columns at the entry, and the exposed-aggregate concrete front stoop.

LIGHT AND CALM. The double-height window slot carved into the dropped ceiling helps scoop light into the space. Minimizing the number of upper cabinets ensures a clean open look, while the careful attention paid to coordinating natural wood finishes helps to make this inherently active space a calm refuge. [above]

KITCHEN. Simple wood cabinets set casually between high-tech appliances and stock windows create an informal sense of craftsmanship, while the dropped ceiling over the cooking area helps define the kitchen as separate from the cathedral-ceilinged great room. [facing page]

Making the Free Line Affordable

WHEN INCORPORATING A CURVED WALL into square construction, the best way to keep costs down is to make the wall non-load-bearing. The layout of the curve is much tougher when these walls also contain columns. In this house, the curved wall is merely a screen set below a by-passing roof made from trusses independently supported by remote columns, an approach that made this grand gesture affordable—almost an architectural Robin Hood scenario of saving money on one end and spending it on another.

The curve was gentle enough to accept the straight lines of the doors and windows that are set within it, and the flat stock trim could be bent to the gentle curves without having to be custom milled to the actual curving shape. Vertical siding easily clads a curving wall as well. The ideal and the real shake hands, and a potentially discordant assemblage of spaces is given a common heart.

The one extraordinary customized gesture is the unforgettable spiraling central wall and courtyard that binds all parts of this house together. Made less expensive by the use of standard materials and simplified layout methods, this curving showstopper is visible from almost every part of the interior, and it bleeds directly into the landscape, which means it can be appreciated by everyone who uses the house on a daily basis.

Necessity is the mother of invention, but it is only through the inventive use of inexpensive materials and standard building techniques that so much customization became affordable. Given all the extra spaces and uses, cost had to be factored into every decision.

For about the same amount of money, this family could have opted for a bloated 5,000-sq.-ft. spec house to accommodate their unique living situation. But that wasn't for them. When you design a house to fit specific occupants, it is typically true that more money is spent per square foot, but the total square footage that you build can shrink to provide that fit. Such "fit" is impossible in the undesigned sea of boxes most housing consumers get to choose from. If this family can create a home that fits them on a budget that competes with that sea of sprawl, there's hope for anyone who wants more than what is usually offered.

MASTER BEDROOM. A carefully sized recess makes room for a prized piece of furniture, while interior doors open onto a small office. [left]

GREAT ROOM TO KITCHEN. Kitchen tile transitions to wood floor, zigzagging out to accommodate the column and wood stove, and forms a visual separation between living and cooking spaces. The wood stove has a full masonry heat shield set behind and below it. [bottom left]

ENTRY. Judicious use of fieldstone creates a focal point in this craftsmanly façade. Stock windows form the lintel between the two stone piers, framed by simple dimensional-lumber knee braces that support all the gable-end roofs. [facing page]

STAIRWAY. The straight-run stairs that lead up to the children's bedrooms above the garage use closed-stringer steps, square balusters, and stock railings to save money without a sense of penny-pinching. [above]

FRONT FAÇADE. The house presents two three-story gable forms to the street, with distinctively painted projecting bays. These towers are set on a solid concrete base that has channels (or "reveals") cast into its face to take the edge off its potentially raw appearance.

Uphill Battle

IT'S GETTING HARDER AND HARDER TO FIND A GREAT SITE
in America's suburbs. Almost all the good properties—those with beautiful exposures, easy access, favorable grade and subsoil conditions in established neighborhoods—already have something built on them. As a result, "tear-downs" have now become commonplace, and houses are regularly bought for their site, demolished, and replaced with a new house.

Chris and Janelle Owens and their three children desperately wanted to build a new home within the city limits of Seattle. What they found was an alternative to the classic tear-down. Their site was close to town and had terrific views of Lake Washington, but the quarter-acre lot had soil so spongy no one had the courage to build on it, and a 21-in. drainpipe from a nearby golf course ran through it. To top it all off, one portion of the site had grades in excess of 40 percent slope (even 15 percent is deemed tough by most builders). One benefit of the slope was that it allowed for an additional 7 ft. 8 in. of height over the normal 30-ft. zoning limitation.

● ● ● **THE CONNECTION.** On the uphill-facing back side of the house, a cantilevered standing-seam shed roof connects the twin gables. [top right]

LIVING ROOM TO BACK PATIO. Careful juxtaposition of natural wood eave undersides and pine doors complements the concrete paving and lush gardens. In the distance, a wall of large boulders forms the last level of earth retainage on the site. [top left]

DRY BED. A stone "stream" leads up to a golf course above the house. [bottom]

BURIED TREASURE

Clearly, the site was going to take a lot of work before the Owens could build on it. Whereas a foundation on a benign lot might cost 10 percent to 15 percent of any given building budget, the foundation and site work for this house approached one-third of the construction budget (see the sidebar on p. 92). It entailed building a 100-ft.-long shoring wall supported by 21 steel flange piles, driving 10 auger-cast piles at least 30 ft. below grade, and constructing 5 separate landscape retaining walls to hold back the hillside. Given all this engineering, the full 15-percent-plus design fee is quite reasonable.

To compensate for this large chunk of equity being eaten by something no one will ever see, architects Brian Brand and Ed Sozinho of Baylis Architects sought to make the house smaller than the 4,000 sq. ft. the owners originally thought they needed for a five-bedroom home. They designed the home to be easy to build (from the ground up, at least) despite its visual variety. The ingenious simplicity of the house construction is evidenced by the fact that the final cost per foot (excluding the foundation) was about $116 in 2001, an exceptional value given the time and place. This home is a classic dance between saving money by using standard materials and the vision of creative architects dealing with limits.

BOXED SET

Although the architect refers to the house as "two pods connected by a central circulation core," the owners' main desire was to

● ●● **FROM THE KITCHEN SINK.** A light-grabbing, two-sided projection off the basic box of the house captures a broad view of the lake. Cabinets and trim are suitably simple so as not to compete with the view.

MIDDLE FLOOR

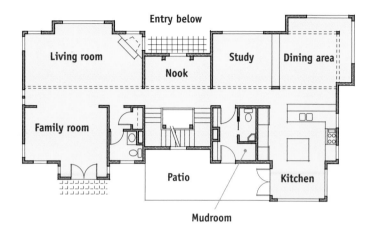

Living room

Entry below

Study

Dining area

Nook

Family room

Patio

Mudroom

Kitchen

FLOOR PLANS

The simple one-two-three layout of flanking square "towers" and their joining piece (the stair/entry/center hallway) make for consistency between all three levels of construction. Additionally, the two beams that link all three of these components together are aligned for maximum structural efficiency. Functionally, the ground floor takes care of business (cars, entry, mechanical), the middle floor gathers people for eating and socializing, and the top floor gives them rest with sleeping and bathroom spaces, all connected by the consistent center stairwell.

TOP FLOOR

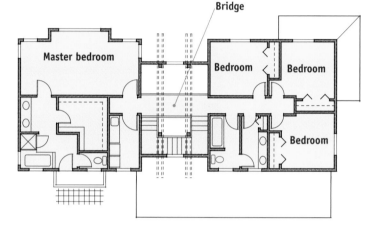

Bridge

Master bedroom

Bedroom

Bedroom

Bedroom

create a reinvention of the Craftsman style. The house is organized around two square boxes or towers about 25 ft. on each side that are connected by a central stairwell. This in-between space is no dark and gloomy stairway, but rather a soaring event of space, light, and material that allows a full three-story house to be elegantly interconnected. The columns that join all three floors have an unbroken height of 33 ft. (which would have been highly problematic with natural wood but was very doable with an engineered wood product called parallel-strand lumber).

The stair itself is formed with closed stringers with slab treads butt-jointed to them—one of the least expensive approaches to stair detailing. The added benefit is that this central stairway kept the total area devoted to hallways and stairs down to less then 10 percent of the house area—a very efficient ratio given that stock plans often devote 15 percent to 20 percent of a house's available space to hallways and stairs.

The vertical organization makes it possible for the house to have a very simple lateral layout. The ground floor takes care of business (cars, entry, mechanical) and also provides guest room and play space. The middle level has all the common spaces, including the kitchen, family room, living room, dining area, half-bath, and mudroom. The top floor is left for family bedrooms, nicely split with parents occupying one tower as a full master suite (including laundry) and the three kids' bedrooms each taking a corner of the other tower. A common kids' bathroom stakes

Location:	Seattle, Washington
Year Built:	2001
Architects:	Brian Brand and Ed Sozinho, Baylis Architects
Finished Heated Space:	3,800 sq. ft.
Costs:	$643,000 ($200,000 for foundation costs)
	Site Development—$75,000
	Design Fee—$110,000

It's less expensive to celebrate raw structu

THIRD FLOOR. Flanked by steel railings on either side, a wood bridge connects the master bedroom suite in one tower with the children's bedrooms in the other. [left]

CENTRAL STAIR TOWER. Wood, drywall, and steel are bathed in light from oversized windows. The columns, which are an engineered wood product called parallel-strand lumber, ascend a full 33 ft. to the ceiling, which would have been a formidable challenge using dimensional lumber. [top right]

BASEMENT LEVEL. Low walls make the bottom of the stair even more affordable than the steel railings used elsewhere. The floor at this level is polished, uncolored concrete. [bottom right]

han to hide it under drywall or trim.

Crafty Use of Cheap Materials

A LITTLE CAREFUL DETAILING can give inexpensive materials the look and feel of finely crafted construction.

PLYWOOD. There's no cheaper surface material than plywood, and this house utilizes plywood that is normally used for sign material: medium-density overlay (MDO), which has an impregnated paper skin for perfectly flat exterior surfaces.

CEMENT BOARD SIDING is often used for institutional buildings (you see it all the time in gas stations). The product is essentially concrete sheet stock that has fibers cast into it for tensile strength.

CONCRETE is cheap, but it can look fairly rough. In this case, the architects had pieces of wood set into the forms for the concrete prior to pouring, which allowed for visual shadow lines to be created. This procedure produced a foundation reminiscent of large-scale blocks of stone.

ENGINEERED WOOD products use the least expensive wood available (scraps) and process it to create a stable building material. These products were once seen as virtually industrial in nature, but this house shows that they can be carefully cut, sanded, and finished.

out the fourth corner. Careful design of the bathrooms segregated sinks from toilet rooms so they could be used by more than one person at a time.

THINKING INSIDE AND OUTSIDE THE BOXES

Structurally, the above-grade house is built with stock materials, often with components exposed as design features. Boxes are easy to build, and these have a few columns in their center to hold up the floor and one steel beam to avoid a column in the garage. The engineered-wood columns and beams (made of large chips of wood glued and compressed together) were stained and finished rather than drywalled over and are featured throughout the stairwell and all the ceilingscapes, as well as under the eaves and porch roofs.

The exterior is clad mostly in painted cement board board-and-batten siding, a product that, although it can be harder to install than wood, is much less expensive. The bay projections were sided in MDO (medium-density overlay) smooth-faced plywood pieced together with exposed seams that use their ¼-in. joints as a design feature. This inexpensive plywood siding is made more durable by using a high-tech coating rather than standard house paint. Clear cedar clapboard is reserved for the focal connecting piece between the two towers. Simple stock aluminum gutters and aluminum-frame windows lend a crisp counterpoint to the natural wood background and rich colors.

SYMPHONY OF MATERIALS. Natural wood spans between painted board-and-batten siding, while the standing-seam aluminum roof serves as a counterpoint to the gabled forms.

LIVING ROOM. An inexpensive stock wood-burning firebox utilizes a custom-painted cement board shroud and polished steel flue for custom impact amid the contrasting painted drywall and open wood structure.

"Ugly duckling" sites can become affordable swans

When a Tough Site Is Worth the Effort

THERE'S ONLY ONE REASON TO SPEND fully 30 percent of your construction budget on your foundation—because the location and views are worth it. For this house, three remedies made a bad site buildable:

- Retain a lot of earth to facilitate construction on a steeply sloping site. The builders did this with rock and concrete retaining walls, and 110 ft. of steel pilings with their ends cast in concrete.

- Provide for drainage by rerouting an existing 21-in. pipe and redirecting the subsurface groundwater with a rigorous system of collecting pipes. Surface water was intercepted and headed off at the top of the site.

- Hold up the house on poor subsoil with concrete auger piles, taking the house's weight down to sound subsoil 30 ft. below grade.

Once all the ground work had been done, the rest of the house was essentially a conventional building, and one built with a cost-consciousness that was a direct result of all the money that had been buried.

A simple asphalt shingle roof is used for the towers (an inexpensive surface for an area that is seldom seen), while more expensive standing-seam aluminum is used for the high-visibility low-pitched connector, patio roof, and saddlebag extensions.

The site developments are as interesting and expressive as the house's shape and construction. A large cantilevered roof floats over the backyard patio and is accompanied by similar trellises, balconies, and rooflets, all utilizing 2x rafters set upon parallel-strand timbers. Wraparound terraces created by the retaining walls at the back side of the house nestle up to the hillside, and a wonderful meandering stone path serves as a visual "stream" up to a hilltop golf course and view.

SIMPLE STYLE

Given all the costs that went underground, the cabinetry and interior detailing are relatively straightforward. Countertops are plastic laminate, and all cabinets were purchased from the discount chain IKEA®. Doors are of the simplest variety available—flush, solid core, with basic flat stock trim surrounding all openings. A prefabricated firebox is used in the living room, and stock steel tubing forms balusters and newels that zoom up the full three-floor run of stairs.

It would have been a lot easier to simply take the $200,000 concrete base and plop a stock plan onto it and appreciate the views. But these owners chose designers and a builder (Douglas Johnson) who literally rose to the challenge of making a house that took advantage of its elevated perch. The home's dramatic exterior is anything but predictable, and the carefully laid out interior allows for the ease of living that is essential for contemporary family life. It's not enough to take financial risks when building a house. The risks taken to go boldly where no stock plan has gone before allow this ugly duckling of a lot's house to soar above its site's buried defects.

THE KITCHEN. Inexpensive stock cabinets rise above the ordinary with a narrow soffit connection above and carefully positioned windows below. The large windows employed in the bay and the bare beam between the bay and the kitchen make a boxy space come alive without intricate detailing and materials. [above left]

FRONT DOOR. An oasis of wood amid a sea of concrete and paint creates a human-scaled element in a big façade. The simply crafted trellis and aluminum gutters are used to reinforce this focal point. [above right]

FLOOR AND RAIL DETAILS. Oriented strand timbers combine with natural pine flooring and simple painted steel fasteners and railings to create a functional yet aesthetic display of the various parts that are often buried in standard home construction. [left]

FROM BACK TO FRONT. The second floor is supported by painted steel columns that lead the eye through the house. The angled walls almost look curved in this sweeping view, while a simple level change at the bottom of the stairs allows the home's floor level to respond to the sloping site.

Sculpture on the Slide

SOMETIMES AN UNCONVENTIONAL SITE FINDS AN UNUSUAL HOUSE.

Turner Brooks and his wife, fellow architect Eeva Pelkonen, discovered just such a site. Its high point was at the street edge and its sloping shape spread out from the street to a flattened area, a site which had no real charm or sense of place.

A classic developer's response to such a potentially disappointing piece of real estate would be to make it fit a stock plan by bringing in truckload after truckload of fill, using the house as a virtual earth dam, with its broad side fronting the street and an ungainly two-and-a-half- or three-story mass facing a sad (and relatively inaccessible) back yard. Rather than turn their house into a wall, Turner and Eeva opted to make a slithering slide of a house that goes with the flow of the site rather than trying to fight it. The design arose from a series of faxes and e-mails during a one-month intercontinental design dialogue between Connecticut and Finland (Eeva's home before marrying Turner). The result is a three-bedroom, two-bath house that effectively conquers the sloping ⅛ acre of land.

●●● **THE SLIDE DOWN THE HILL.** Using one vertical bend amidships (seen at the vertical mullion in the lone custom-built diagonal window) and one bend of the roof plane (just uphill of the break in the wall plane), this basic palette of materials has enough quirky flow to be at once sculptural and tongue-in-cheek. [above]

FACING THE STREET. Almost enigmatically simple, this box with various-sized holes cut into its sides challenges the viewer to figure out what's going on inside. The stark use of generic materials contrasts nicely with the power line hook-up, highlighting its sinuous quality. [above left]

BACKSIDE. As the roof tilts down and the walls bend around, the shed dormer launches upward and the cascading steps flow forth from the back side, bridging the gap between the open floor within and the grade. [above right]

GREAT SHAPE FROM AN ODD LOT

The lot is in downtown New Haven on an old utility road originally built to provide access for carriages serving the 19th-century mansions that surround it. Due to its humble pedigree, the site's width, slope, and orientation were intended more for no-frills accommodation than for bucolic site design. Such oddball lots present a good opportunity for inexpensive ugly ducklings to become the swans of the neighborhood. Being in a city, the site had full sewer, water, and utility hookups in the street, bringing site development costs to a paltry $1,500.

The house is built with standard dimensional lumber and other conventional materials, but it gets its dramatic form from a few walls that are skewed out of square. The roof has no peaks or valleys (which saves money), and with one exception, all the windows are stock and rectilinear. Siding is 4-in. painted clapboard, the most generic, least expensive, solid-wood exterior surface. Interior finishes are similarly off the rack—painted drywall or exposed plywood.

If there were no photographs with this description, you might think this a simple, perhaps even predictable, building where cost constraints and site design limitations were obvious. However, the photos tell the tale of a house that seems to have a life of its own, sitting sphinxlike on its backyard site. Responding to the site's skewed outline and sliding terrain, the lightly angled side

In the world of right-angled construction, a few odd angles give big bang for the buck.

Safety in Whole Cloth

NEW PARENTS ARE UNDERSTANDABLY CONCERNED about protecting their babies from themselves, and, in this case, a little baby in an open house required extraordinary protection. Here, simple canvas stretched tight at the edge of the stair opening uses a crafty cable stay system whose points of attachment are on display at eye level as you go up and down the stair. The upside of this system is that once danger wanes as the years go by, the canvas can be removed. In the meantime, its bright yellow countenance serves as a marvelous center of color for a simple yet expressive home.

DOWN THE STAIR. With the master bedroom beyond to the left and the living room down the stairs to the right, the ubiquitous fir ceiling, stock doors, and wood floors make for an active interior with stock parts. The consistent use of materials keeps chaos at bay, but whimsy is clearly in evidence as ceilings and walls bend and move to some unheard rhythm. [above left]

FROM THE SECOND-FLOOR HALLWAY. The diagonal window that faces south directly over the stairs, a single custom element in a sea of standard parts, defines the crease in the wall that gives this home its three-dimensional appeal as seen from the outside and provides critical light at the very center of the plan. [left]

Sometimes it takes a different house to fit a different site.

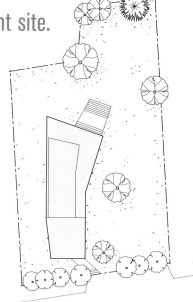

SITE PLAN

By setting the house tight to the street and to the northern property line of this tiny lot, the one gently sloped area (right) was left undeveloped.

FLOOR PLANS

A simple recessed entry leads to an ever-widening flow of space into the backyard-facing living/dining/kitchen area (left). Four columns provide support for the second floor, with the first three lining up like good soldiers but the last one stepping out of alignment to follow the splayed wall. The second floor (right) takes care of the family bedrooms and office.

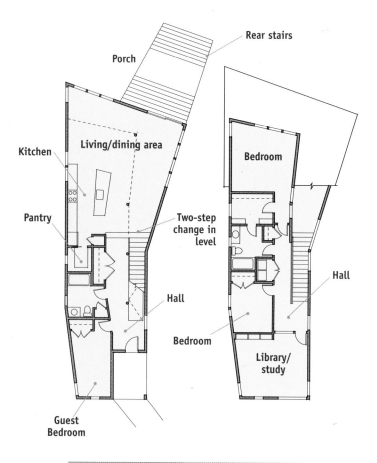

Porch

Rear stairs

Kitchen

Living/dining area

Pantry

Two-step change in level

Hall

Hall

Bedroom

Bedroom

Library/ study

Guest Bedroom

Location:	**New Haven, Connecticut**
Year Built:	2000
Architect:	Turner Brooks, Eeva Pelkonen
Finished Heated Space:	1,820 sq. ft.
Costs:	Project Budget—$247,000
	Site Development—$1,500

wall seems to "flow" down the landscape—allowing this home to have its own unique shape rather than that of a traditional home that's meant to sit level and square to the site.

ACTIVE ON THE INSIDE

In terms of layout, the house is as simple as the parts it's made of. Once you come inside through the recessed entry (bypassing a guest bedroom), you walk through an open hallway past closets, bath, and pantry to a two-step drop down that extends the main stair into the living area. The stair itself, made of steel and wood, has open risers that both reveal a view through the house and filter it at the same time. Once at the lower level, a light-filled kitchen, dining, and living area opens up to the backyard. Upstairs, the master bedroom takes full advantage of the view. A central bathroom and laundry serve both the guest bedroom and the relatively large library/study that's set above the entry and the guest bedroom below. This second floor takes up only about two-thirds of the first-floor area, leaving double-height space at the stair and over the living area.

The interior detailing is powerfully simple. Steel columns follow the line of the stair, except for one that steps out of line where the back of the house splays open to the backyard. Kitchen cabinets are green-stained birch veneer plywood, without ornament other than the highlighted grain. The backsplash is a full span of ceramic mosaic tile, and the countertops are plastic laminate with a stock aluminum edge, all low-cost kitchen material

Simple Ceilings

DRYWALL IS NOT THE ONLY OPTION when choosing an inexpensive wall or ceiling surface. Here, using one of the cheapest materials available (AC plywood) provides a little variety at minimal cost. Openly displaying its 4x8 panel module (with no applied trim or detailing to hide the joints), this unfinished raw material stands in stark contrast to the painted drywall it butts up against.

KITCHEN CABINET. When care and contrast are employed strategically, generic elements become almost poetic. The kitchen cabinets [below] are a combination of stock elements, including stained fronts, stainless-steel handles, aluminum counter edge, ceramic mosaic tiles, and plastic-laminate top. [above right]

ENTRY STAIR. A minimalist custom stair that embodies the elemental aesthetic properties of wood and metal draws attention to itself through its unmistakably diagonal presence. Painted steel columns offset the birch floor in a classic duet of color and natural material. [above]

KITCHEN. Green-stained birch cabinets and industrial lighting let the materials speak for themselves. The splayed island countertop reflects the angling of the living/dining area and the house in general. [facing page]

selections. A walk-in pantry gives the kitchen a functional utility beyond that conveyed by the minimal cabinetry.

Windows are used in a variety of ways. A lone oddball diagonal window sits alongside the stair and is split by the crotch corner of the long south wall, highlighting the crease. The light from the large window in the second-floor library/study flows through an interior glass wall at the top of the stair, backlighting the entire space. Low interior windows in the master bedroom open into the stair space, providing ventilation and an unexpected visual connection to the living/dining area.

FOOTING THE BILL

Cost played a critical role in the design of this home. Almost all the materials used came out of the local hardware store catalog, and, given that the owners were the designers, there was no design fee. But ultimately, the biggest factor in helping this house stay on budget was keeping its bulk and square footage down. And because the house's 63½ ft. of length and over 20 ft. of overall height are almost completely open, there's no sense that the house is at all cramped.

At $124/sq. ft. in the year 2000, the cost of the house is well below that of comparable custom-built homes and competitive with stock-plan construction costs. Unbound by preconceptions, Turner Brooks and Eeva Pelkonen wrought every angle and quirk, and this site virtually hugs those twists and turns. Because it rejects a predictable plan, shape, or detailing to respond to its awkward site, this home celebrates both its occupants and its context, and like all good sculpture, the happy result is there for all to see.

ENTRY PAVILION. One of four "cabinettes," this pavilion is an artful distillation of careful craftsmanship. The small pavilion captures the essence of the cabin in the woods that was the site's original context and serves to inspire its new inhabitants.

Cabins in the Woods

NO ONE WOULD ACCUSE LISTON AND CORINNE TATUM OF BEING PREDICTABLE thinkers. In the 1950s, they built a classic glass house" one of pristine modernist appeal. Now, in what is supposed to be their retirement, they opted to build yet another house, this one set in the Maryland countryside. If they'd followed the well-worn path of their peers, they might have picked a Gold Coast retirement community condominium. Instead they opted to buy a building lot in a wooded community called Scientists Cliffs high above Chesapeake Bay. The original buildings of this community, which was founded as a summer colony in 1935, were tiny cabins constructed of solid chestnut logs. Wayne Good, the local architect the Tatums hired, was inspired by the context to make a house of four small, connected shapes, each about the size of an original Scientists Cliffs cabin.

The best of residential architecture allows for personal expression both for the owners and for the architect. As Good began to talk to the Tatums about their site's history and took their thoughts to heart, they knew this design process would be different from their first go-round with homebuilding, where context and owner input took a backseat to a dramatic final product. Empowered by

● ● ● **HANDRAIL.** A brass pipe is a natural contrast to the faux log siding at the stairway side. [top left]

ENTRY STAIR. With a full wall of glass to the left and the low wall of "logs" to the right, the view at the top of the stairs offers a wonderful sense of contrast. Complementing this is the trimless opening in the wall, which gives a peek-a-boo view to the living space for those going downstairs. [above]

LIVING ROOM APPROACH. As seen from the entry/stair hall, the white wall serves as screen and threshold to the living room, creating the sense that this is a processional entry with a nice level of anticipatory buildup. [top right]

the partnership, the Tatums received what they like to call a "subliminal boost" from the design of their house.

LITTLE CABINS MAKE A HOUSE

The first goal of the architect was to re-create some of the sensibilities of the original 1930s compound—not quite in the manner of the chestnut logs of the original summer colony, but with an iconic sensibility. With that attitude as his starting point, Good created a string of wooden beads that tame a rolling landscape into a safe harbor. The four "cabinettes" provide 2,800 sq. ft. of space organized to reflect the various activities of the occupants.

Free thinkers as they are, the Tatums did *not* opt for the classic one-level retirement home. This is truly a two-story house, but one that allows for a full-functioning lifestyle with the upper level of the four cabins set to the level of car access, comprising the entries, a complete master bedroom suite, dining room/kitchen, and the living area. Below this, guest spaces open out into the light and air that a sloping site affords lower levels. Although the house is quite large for a two-bedroom, two-bath house, the variety of social spaces makes it possible to accommodate a large number of guests (which is always a good thing in empty-nester homes).

Three of the four cabins have a relatively classic shape, utilizing a 90-degree roof angle (what architects and builders call a 12-in-12 pitch) clad in asphalt shingles. The fourth cabin is an overtly

ENTRY PAVILION THRESHOLD. Using the simplest of materials, this entry gives a glimpse into the sheltered interior of the house while providing direct connection to the outdoor world. Almost poetic in its capture of construction technique, this pavilion is both distinct from the landscape and completely open to it—very much like the hunting lodges found in this part of the world.

The Big Picture

BIG VIEWS NEED BIG WINDOWS. Here, the architect used double-hung units (the least expensive kind of operable glass) to create windows that are approximately 8 ft. tall and 3 ft. wide. At this large scale, the windows align with the 8-ft.-high standard doors on the upper floor that open onto the deck. The windows are "mulled" directly together (rather than having their separate frames set in walls) and are unified by trim that wraps around their full combined perimeter. They come relatively close to the floor, which means the glass must be tempered, increasing the cost, but the overall effect, especially set within the tall cathedral ceiling spaces of this house, adds punch to the largest space in the house.

In the Words of ●●●

Howard Freeman, Freeman Builders

"To build a house is a job. To create a well-crafted home is a pleasure. It is a satisfying creative process, involving the input of all participants: client, architect, and builder with staff and subcontractors. We work together to achieve a level of craftsmanship, art, grace, and style that fills one with a sense of well-being and beauty. We built a home for the Tatums that made sense. It fit their needs without being ostentatious, flowery, or overstated. The joinery is tight, the paint lines true, rooms are square, finishes are clean, direct, and honest. The little things matter; they make up the whole."

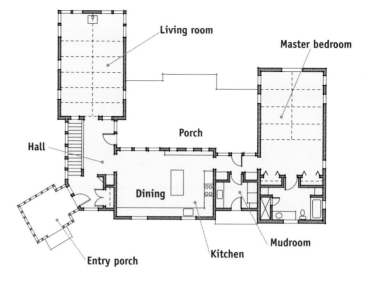

FIRST-FLOOR PLAN

Four boxes are connected by three parts, including the rear deck that provides common outdoor space. The stairs lead down to the basement level, with family room, crafts room, and guest bedroom.

SOUTH-SIDE ELEVATION

Tucked in amongst mature trees, the house is set tight to the street (at right) and extends to a full two stories as the site slopes gently to the back. The entry pavilion is at far right.

Location:	Scientists Cliffs, Port Republic, Maryland
Year Built:	1998
Architect:	Wayne L. Good, FAIA, Good Architecture
Finished Heated Space:	2,800 sq. ft.
Costs:	Project Budget—$310,000
	Site Development—$40,000
	Design Fee—$65,000

symbolic entry pavilion that has a preformed metal roof with an open stickwork structure—all set at an angle to command the attention of anyone entering the site.

Even though the four different cabins have consistent rooflines, window types, and detailing, the siding has some subtle differences. At first glance, most of the siding appears to be classic board-and-batten wood siding, but although natural wood is used for the battens (the vertical strips), plywood is used for the boards to save money. Two types of this faux board-and-batten siding are employed. The majority is inexpensive AC plywood with a grainy wood veneer surface, while at the "living cabin" the siding set between the expansive windows is made of MDO (medium-density overlay) plywood, normally a sign-making material, its smooth face used to contrast the rough cedar trim and battens. Plywood is used to face the soffits as well, but the eaves have a projecting beam, or "outrigger," added to their square profile, creating an extra level of detail and shadow line. As a paean to the log homes of the 1930s, the architect used faux log siding (rounded and milled solid-cedar clapboards) on selected areas.

TWIN GASKETS

Two carefully designed connecting pieces allow all the individual forms to function together as a single house. One, at the front door, interconnects three of these different shapes (entry, living,

space at ground level.

MASTER BEDROOM SITTING AREA. Generous space makes this bedroom more than just a sleeping place. All windows are standard, but ganging together double-hung windows with fixed transoms allows their scale to fit the vaulted ceiling. The wood floor, collar ties, and furniture provide a nice complement to the painted drywall. [left]

BACK SIDE. Walls made of rough siding contrast with walls made of smooth plywood at the living room (right). The master bedroom wing (left) has similar battens but uses the rougher-faced veneer plywood for its board surface. These contrasts highlight the multicabin approach and complement the windows used and functions housed—living public, bedroom private. [below]

OUTDOOR TERRACE. "Log" siding is used for the central cabin, while the roughly hewn plywood board-and-batten siding is visible beyond the common deck. [bottom left]

ON THE SLOPE. Three of the four cabinettes are set to the slope, with connecting pieces between them providing access. The standing-seam steel roof used for the entry (and on the unseen connector roofs) contrasts with the asphalt shingle roofing used elsewhere to give each building its own presence.

●●● **UNDER THE EAVES.** Even though the exterior of the house is rustic and all materials are generic, an overall sense of design is expressed in the precise joinery of the extended eaves. [above]

KITCHEN. Custom-crafted maple cabinets and high-tech stainless-steel appliances work together to create a sense of linear and craftsmanly interplay not often seen in a house with this budget. [top, facing page]

FROM THE ENTRY. The centerline of the living room is reinforced by the position of the windows, including the openings in the interior wall, and by the powerful presence of the woodstove and its backdrop. [bottom, facing page]

and kitchen), and as such its roof form is low, has multiple pitches, and is roofed with sheet metal to prevent leaks. The second "gasket" serves as the mudroom, back door, and laundry room, connects the kitchen and master bedroom cabins, and provides direct access from the outside through to the deck beyond.

Aside from the functional segregation and siding types, the cabins have distinctive ceilingscapes inside. A flat ceiling sits above the kitchen and dining area; a cathedral ceiling (with naturally finished fir collar ties set 4 ft. apart) over the living room has the scale of a gathering place; the master bedroom suite has a cathedral ceiling as well over its sleeping area while its bathroom area has a flat ceiling; and the entry has an open-framed ceiling that fully exposes the various layers and materials used.

AVOIDING CABIN FEVER

Simple right-angle construction using standard materials allowed this project to be executed for a relatively low price, but there were some places where money was spent with gusto. The kitchen is an array of maple cabinetry and high-tech appliances. Most floors are natural wood. Although windows are stock, there are quite a few of them, ganged together to make walls of glass. And the entry itself is a true confection of construction, not a necessity. Even the HVAC system ducts are carefully laid out to coincide with various openings and adjacencies (rather than

A little bit of whimsy goes a long way when it's located for maximum exposure.

The Entry Pavilion

THE DISTINCTIVE ENTRY PAVILION shows how simple framing techniques and materials can be carefully combined to create an architectural statement that is both familiar and energized—very much in the best tradition of residential design. Set on piers rather than integrated into the home's basement, this housebound folly is a three-dimensional diagram of construction techniques, using subtle tricks that make it as much crafty sculpture as building.

The pavilion is built using 2x4 studs set 12 in. on center (shrinking the standard 16-in. module), and the eave overhangs are reduced to half the size of those found on the rest of the house. A full wraparound of the faux log siding bands the pavilion's base, which is precisely mitered to create a plinth. The whole effect is of a visual signpost in the woods—miniaturized, kicked at an angle, with abstract detailing to draw the eye.

● ● ● **ENTRY PAVILION FROM THE INSIDE.** A doorway and a large fixed-glass panel provide visual access to the entry pavilion, revealing the wonderful interplay of light, line, and material.

being laid out simply to serve the spaces they feed). Similarly, trim is carefully coordinated to provide around-the-room alignment.

In digging into the hillside, approximately 20 percent of the total building budget was dedicated to taming the contours. In creating and describing so many carefully detailed and coordinated surfaces, shapes, and spaces, the architect's fee ended up being more than 15 percent of the construction budget—at the higher end of most residential design fee structures. Without this level of design and craftsmanship, the home could not hope to combine so many shapes, spaces, and materials with such thoughtful detailing. Of course, some homeowners might not have wanted so much from an architect, and some architects might not have delivered such a wonderfully crafted home. When design opportunities are met with inspired skill, the hearts and minds of the home's occupants are freed to take on the rest of life. For these owners, this home is more than a dream, it is the nesting place for a long life lived together.

●●● **FROM MASTER BEDROOM THROUGH KITCHEN TO ENTRY.** By carefully aligning the openings between rooms, the overall sense of space in the house is greatly enhanced. The faux log siding at the stairwell is a direct reference to the exterior siding.

FROM BELOW. A central steel support runs the length of the house, while the rafters that form the long single-pitched sloping roof announce themselves with similar vigor. Color applied to the cement-board panel siding makes this smooth, generic material a rich counterpoint to the wood-filled interior.

Light and Line

GEORGE AND SUE GOSLINE HAD A CLEAR VISION OF WHAT THEY WANTED

for their new home. After 33 years of marriage and raising a family, they needed a simpler, smaller place to live that would free them of the maintenance woes of their existing house and allow them to welcome back adult children. And they knew they wanted a house designed by architect Peter Bohlin, an architect with a clear vision of what a house should be. Like all projects, but especially those intended to reduce a family's cost of living, this house had a specific budget. The Goslines and Bohlin approached this project with two basic mind-sets about keeping costs down.

First, they had (and took) the time to get it right—it took a year and a half from initiating the design to breaking ground. While it might seem that more time would translate to greater cost, in fact the reverse is true. Time allows you to put price tags on all the features of a design and judge whether any given material, element, or space is worth its portion of the money available. When time is pressed, people tend to build more square footage and include features that would be winnowed out if there were time to cost out options before construction begins. Second, all parties (including builder Eric Thorsen) were open to using standard stock materials in nontraditional ways.

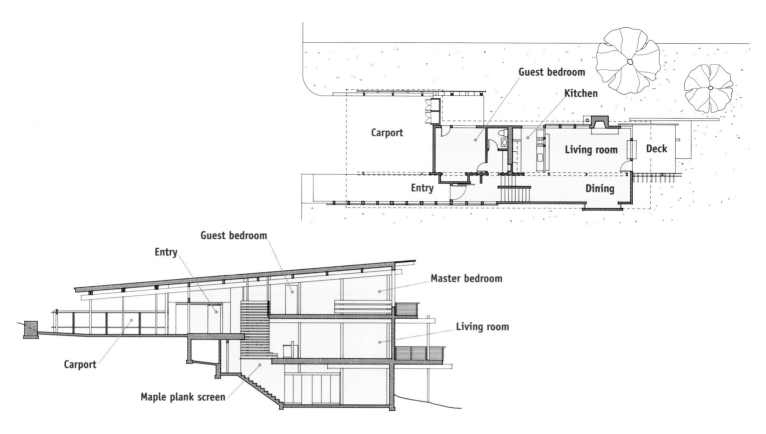

SITE AND FIRST-FLOOR PLAN

At street level, a large carport forms one side of an entry, while the house extends out to the street. The kitchen is tucked in overlooking the view, and the living room space extends to form a deck beyond. The projecting bay allows more space for the dining area.

CROSS SECTION

As the single pitched roof launches up, the ground plane cascades down. The entry is set at the half-level between the lofted master bedroom and the lower living spaces below it. The lowest level houses the guest bedroom and has access out to the street.

Location:	**Seattle, Washington**
Year Built:	2000
Architect:	Bohlin, Cywinski, Jackson
Finished Heated Space:	2,100 sq. ft.
Costs:	Project Budget—withheld
	Site Development—withheld
	Design Fee—withheld

THE SHAPE OF THINGS TO COME

To build this home designed for the next phase of their lives, the Goslines had purchased a corner lot on a steeply sloping site. Located in Seattle, the site itself was only 50 ft. wide and 120 ft. long—just a little bit over ⅛ acre in size. The resulting 2,100-sq.-ft. house virtually had its 19-ft. 8-in. width and 50-ft. length determined by the shape of the site. There was nothing remarkable about the basic design criteria (a 3-bedroom, 2½-bath empty nester house) or the materials used to fabricate it. What is remarkable is the result: a house that combines these generic materials in a design that evokes a sense of hand-sculpted architecture.

The simple plan layout is made overtly architectural by exposing all the structure that normally lurks behind the drywall. Those parts that are normally hidden are exposed and fully expressed in the cantilevered porches that face the downhill view.

OUTSIDE IN

The home's linear plan uses the site's slope to create an expansive interior. On the uphill side of the site, a carport (cheaper than a garage) starts an entry sequence that transitions effortlessly from

Leaving off-the-rack materials exposed can be less expensive than hiding structure behind

● ● ● **FACING BACK TO THE KITCHEN.** The central spine of steel runs the length of the house, with the rhythmically placed floor joists projecting back from the double-height space. Huge fixed-glass panels are set directly between columns and a fireplace (right), with polished concrete flooring underfoot.

finished surfaces.

●●● **FIREPLACE ON THE SIDE.** On the downhill side, fireplaces are cantilevered off the long wall of the house with their flues projecting up and beyond the eave, which frees up interior space. Facing the view, the transparent corner windows break the box of the house's shape.

● ○ ● **ENTRY SEQUENCE.** Plastic panels set in cedar frames form a slot amid the cement board sheet stock, helping to create an entry sequence that builds anticipation and provides shelter prior to getting inside the house. . The photo on the facing page shows the view from the top of the master bedroom stairs back to the entry. [top and facing page]

FAÇADE DETAIL. Brightly painted colors and exposed battens between the cement sheet stock, wood eaves, and aluminum flashing make this a composition that is as much two-dimensional art as architectural form. [above]

outside to in. A long walkway bordered by cedar frames that support clear plastic panels provides safe harbor and passage to a front door of bubinga (an African wood that's one of the owner's favorites). As you enter the house, the roof slopes up as the grade and floor fall away, allowing you to see down through the main body of the house out to the view while simultaneously seeing up through the upper floor hall to the sky. The home's three bedrooms are set on three separate levels. The master bedroom suite takes over the entire third floor. Discreetly tucked next to the midlevel entry is one guest room, and the lower level is a guest suite. Both guest bedrooms are designed so they can also be used as studies for the owners.

Prefab fireplaces are cantilevered off the long exterior walls, extending into the side yard setback, as is a bay that allows extra space for a dining area on the middle level and a sitting area for the master bedroom above. Similarly, both the master bedroom and the living room have decks that project directly off their space. There are very few doors in this house, with separation provided instead by millwork, changes of level, and the way the spaces are organized.

MATERIAL WORLD

This house is a virtual catalog of building materials, with steel, solid wood, engineered wood, plywood, cement board sheet siding, prefabricated plastic skylight material, and paint combining

Pitched Roofs

ARCHITECT-DESIGNED "MODERN" HOMES often try to resist one of the natural laws of nature (that water flows downhill) by using flat roofs. On this house, the architects had the courage to provide adequate pitch in the rainy world of Washington State by creating a gently sloping one-way roof that is both economical and effective at keeping water away from the inside of the house. This approach is ultimately cost-effective, as it avoids expensive hips and valleys—and flat roofs, over time, inevitably leak more than their pitched counterparts and cost money to repair.

to make a simple form rich in detail. All the materials are generic, but Bohlin has used the contrast between them to create a dynamic display, pushing and pulling the various parts of the exterior surfacing to create some drama between the house's shape, its exposed structure, and the materials themselves. Generic aluminum windows are used as seamless ceiling-to-floor and wall-to-wall glazing—stacked, set side by side, or combined with doors depending on the size of the rooms they sit in, the view they frame, and the tapestry of materials that clad the exterior.

The most generic of flat stock materials, AC plywood (which has one side clear of knots, the other with veneer patches where the knots have been removed) is painted or clear finished and used as a finish material for ceilings and eaves. On the outside, cement board panels are painted in a bold color palette. Steel railings are made of standard tube stock, sheet stock, and wire with standard fittings. There are some custom-crafted details as well, including polished concrete floors for all the common areas. The front door, maple plank partitions, and assorted built-ins provide interior finish work that is sympathetic to the surrounding open structure.

Built-ins and finish trim in the house are designed with gaps between boards and exposed seams and fasteners, making the way these elements are put together as important as their shape

In the Words of ●●●

homeowners George and Sue Gosline

"The design and construction of our 'empty-nest' home was one of the most enjoyable experiences of our lives. We, the architects, and the contractor had a shared vision of craftsmanship and a desire to create a really good building. Perhaps predictably, the only real issue was color. When we questioned the large panels of primary colors, Peter Bohlin was right there to go through hundreds of color swatches with us. He got his way, although the final color is somewhat muted."

...sing contrasting materials and dynamic detailing.

DOUBLE HEIGHT AT THE CORNER. Set at the highest point of the house, the ganged industrial windows ascend to celebrate the double-height space. Deep colors and simple built-ins grace and enrich the room. [above and left]

CONSISTENT DETAILING. Simple maple planks that form the screen between stair runs have an aesthetic connection with the stair treads and the slabs of maple of the kitchen cabinetry. [top]

Let the site organize interior spaces and determine the shape of a home.

DECK DETAILING. Simple materials (steel, wood, and plywood) are allowed to run long, making sculpture out of the necessities of building. [left]

MASTER BEDROOM DECK. With plank flooring leading to gapped decking beyond, door and windows are ganged to form a single fully glazed opening. The natural wood above is set among painted drywall surfaces, while lighting and heating elements (lower right) add energy to the composition. [facing page]

Hidden Comfort

IN HOMES WHERE SO MUCH OF THE STRUCTURE IS EXPOSED, there are two ways to deal with the heating, plumbing, and electrical systems: Either hide them or let them be exposed. In this house, mechanical systems are hidden from view with wires, pipes, and ducts carefully tucked out of sight or behind some of the few fully enclosed wall surfaces. So in a house where money is saved by leaving structure and surface open and unconnected, the rough mechanical equipment is kept under wraps, and a high-art sensibility is meshed with builder-friendly technology to make an affordable product.

and the materials used. The side benefit of this pieces-and-parts style of detailing is that it is cheaper to build than the perfectly joined, flush, and finished millwork typically seen in custom homes.

THE COST OF ART

Peter Bohlin's lively use of basic materials has the happy consequence of being inherently cost-effective, and the overall shape of the house is also penny-wise. A single low-pitched roof angles over the entire house. The three-story split-level construction (with two levels facing the upland side of the hill and three levels facing the view) produces a lot of square footage for the amount of foundation used. The excavation approach also helped keep costs down, given that the fill of the uphill half of the house was essentially supplied by what was cut out for the lower half. And the minimal soil disturbance made it possible to save two of the three mature trees on the site.

While its shape is simple, this is not what you'd call a "quiet" building. Expressing the unique vision of an architect who has spent a career exploring the possibilities of home, this house shows that generic materials can be used in ways that celebrate their surface and shape. It also shows that when client, builder, and designer work with common inspiration, high art can become downright domestic.

STREET SIDE. With small lots surrounding this corner site, the main focus of the home's windows is out over the roadway to the salt marsh beyond. The house is sited on a rocky outcropping, and the linear eave lines with windows arrayed about the chimney and entry (right) transform a gable-ended box into a happy ensemble of well-crafted features.

Angling for Inspiration

FOR MANY AMERICANS, IMPENDING RETIREMENT MEANS MOVING to a senior community, where shared maintenance and close proximity make for easy social contact with a minimum of home-maintenance drudgery. However, this level of demographic consistency isn't for everybody.

Rather than move into such a community, a couple who lived in central Connecticut decided that they would change their life by relocating close to home—but a world away from their classic suburban house. Their search for a change in venue brought them to an extraordinary coastal subdivision on Long Island Sound that had about twenty ⅓-acre sites strung like pearls along a small road system, with more than half the total site acreage held in common.

SMALL SITE, BIG VIEW

The owners chose a corner lot that had lovely distant views over a salt marsh to the south. The lot was elevated 15 ft. above the street on bedrock, allowing the site to stand out amid the density. Building on rock meant that a significant amount of blasting had to occur. However, once this house nestled into the rock, houses that were within 40 ft. of it would be unseen.

ENTRY. By setting the garage doors at an angle, the owners were able to avoid a fair amount of blasting of the bedrock. The simple symmetrical gable of the overarching house form serenely sits above the angular activity. [right]

MASTER BATHROOM. High windows ensure privacy on the side facing neighboring houses, while the low window provides a tubside view over the salt marsh.

Since every cubic inch of blasted granite costs money, it made sense to minimize blasting beyond that needed for a full basement by angling the garage for the most efficient use of the driveway. By setting the garage wing at a 45-degree angle, 20 percent of the blasting needed for site access could be eliminated (and 20 percent more of the wonderful rock outcropping could be preserved).

Beyond access to the site, the owners' needs were very simple. They wanted an open first floor where all rooms save utility spaces (bath, pantry, mudroom, laundry, etc.) would be separated only by cabinetry and low walls. The focal point of this undivided plan is a two-story living area that welcomes those entering the house through the prominent front door. Upstairs, a full master suite has the "catbird seat" of the water view. Additionally, two bedrooms with a shared bath for returning children are located upstairs for maximum privacy, as is a loft office, which is set above the entry overlooking the double-height living space.

MAXIMIZE VALUE, MINIMIZE COST

With all the blasting and angled construction, how could this home be made affordable? The vast majority of the home's structure is a simple rectangular box with a symmetrical gable roof that maximizes the efficiency of its construction. The basic plan

Sometimes it's cheaper to change the house than change the site.

● ● ● **MASTER BEDROOM.** Stock windows arranged in a simple curve expand the master bedroom space by a critical couple of feet at the foot of the bed and also provide a real sense of view perched atop this dramatic site.

Curves Cost, So Use Them Wisely

THERE'S NOTHING QUITE LIKE A CURVE to capture your attention amid the dominant straight lines of construction. In this house, curves are used in places where your eyes naturally go—the entry, the hearth, the stairs, and the view from the master bedroom bed. For the most part, they are also used in ways that are inherently less expensive—it is always easier to cut a flat plane to create a curved edge (like the hearth) than to bend a curve out of the plane of a wall (as with the miniature balcony/landing at the stairway above).

It's easier to create curves from stock elements (like the handrail profile that is made to form the curve at the stair balcony or the flexible plastic trim above the fireplace mantel) than to make something that is totally customized. It's also easier to make curves out of things that fit loosely (like the stone that creates the arching terrace wall) than out of things that are designed to be assembled in straight planes (the windows in the arcing bay of the second-floor master bedroom). So while this house is predominantly rectilinear, it has the spice of the curve to help its focal points grab your attention.

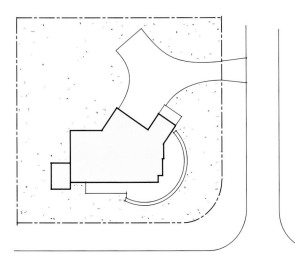

SITE PLAN

Within tight street setbacks, the house is positioned to make the most of the view and to provide the necessary run of driveway to ascend to the site's buildable area. Angling the garage and entry avoided a great deal of blasting and created a compelling counterpoint to the dominant house geometry.

GABLE END. An extended chimney flanked by symmetrical windows is counterbalanced by the corner entry. This angled piece with its outstretched roof reaches out to welcome visitors to the home. [left]

ENTRY PAVILION. A diagonal entry has the power and presence to draw attention away from the garage doors at right and from the large gable roof above. Bending the chimney's brick to the left, gathering in the garage eave to the right, centering its peak on the corner of the main house shape, and providing a simple stepped access to the ground plane pulls together many elements into a definite point of entry. [facing page]

FIRST-FLOOR PLAN

The fireplace/built-in TV unit at the end of the living room dominates the open floor plan, with the stair providing another interior focal point. These large-scale elements balance the extraordinary amount of glass facing the view. The screen porch is easily accessible from the kitchen for undercover dining outside.

Location:	**Coastal Connecticut**
Year Built:	2000
Architect:	Duo Dickinson
Finished Heated Space:	2,900 sq. ft.
Costs:	Project Budget—under $500,000
	Site Development—$30,000±
	Design Fee—$40,000±

was broad enough that the angled two-car garage and entry could be let into its shape without breaking into the gable roof.

A dramatically simple 3-ft. eave overhang was created by extending the rafter tails and integrating them into the house's mass with an angled soffit return—a big bang-for-the-buck detail. Asphalt roof shingles saved money over a wood or metal roof, and all trim used was flat square stock. The owners' choice of Alaskan yellow cedar shingle siding was expensive, but this material has a 40-year lifespan without needing to be painted.

If this were just another gabled box with standard trim, windows, and detailing, there would be very little to recommend it to those walking by in this tightly planned neighborhood. It is in the smaller applied elements that a simple house shape gains life. The owners wanted a masonry fireplace, and it was designed to be a prominent feature inside and out. Rather than a predictably centered traditional chimney, a lightly tapering obelisk of brick rises from a widened base that in turn bends and extends to become a planter. This three-dimensional three-story piece organizes the façade's windows and balances the corner entry in a way that no mere trim or window treatment could have.

The entry itself virtually launches from the corner of the house and is supported by large four-square columns and brackets that grab the attention of everyone entering the site. Around the corner from the chimney lies the house's second grand two-story

The Sum of Stock Parts

THE EXTENDED EAVES OF THIS HOUSE are surfaced with off-the-rack 4-in. painted tongue-in-groove clear cedar. The big brackets that hold up the entry roof utilize a similar tongue-and-groove wood surface executed on a scale that feels comfortable with the overall size of the house and helps to bring the home's mass down to a human scale. The extended chimney is built with common brick that has some painted highlights. Additionally, the low linear roof that cuts across the view side of the house uses painted trim and asphalt shingles to provide a counterpoint to the large façade. None of these elements is unforgettably dramatic, but together, their crafty sensibility makes a simple shape a home.

LIVING ROOM/DINING. The entry is not only turned to greet those coming onto the site but is also set one step above the floor plan, presenting a sweeping, light-filled overview of the house once inside the main living area. [facing page]

HEARTH. With curves for the hearth and the trim above the mantel and windows and cabinetry incorporated into its design, the fireplace has the scale and visual impact to serve as a focal point for this large double-height space.

●●● **OVER THE TERRACE.** This broad two-story façade uses Alaskan yellow cedar siding and white painted trim and eave lines that are nicely contrasted by the variety of windowscaping and the bracket-supported bay. The rooflets over the doors and windows prevent wear and tear from salt water and provide welcome shade in summer.

gesture: a wall of windows that faces out over a terrace to the view, fully acknowledging the double-height space of the living room.

The long line of the home's water-facing façade is highlighted by sun- and rain-shedding rooflets above the first-floor windows and doors, and a second-story set of windows arrayed to form a curved wall. Supporting brackets for these projections give the trim a three-dimensional detailing. At the opposite end of the house, a screen porch butts up against the building and projects its own gable face out toward the view in counterpoint to the dominant lines of the house.

INSIDE LOOKING OUT

Not unlike the exterior of the house, the interior has focal points to prevent predictability and sustain attention. The front door extends into the house in the form of a slightly raised entry platform, with its curving step echoing the curving terrace seen directly outside. The fireplace is the major focal point for the open first floor, with a large curved hearth and trim-cum-mantel, which is coordinated with windows and built-ins for the stereo and TV.

The living area's two-story window wall dominates the double-height room, while a central stair uses standard components with

his usually means the front and entry.

● ○ ● **A BUILDING ON A BUILDING.** The screen porch takes the flat stock trim used throughout the rest of the house and makes it three-dimensional. [above right] Its gable-ended focal point faces the salt marsh and Long Island Sound beyond. [facing page]

INFORMAL DINING. The kitchen island accommodates informal diners and at the same time allows a direct view through the main body of the house. [above]

some careful customization to create a jewel of millwork in the middle of a sea of space. Compensating for the cost of these interior elements, the flooring is ubiquitous 2¼-in. strip oak, and plain trim is used around all openings. All in all, this 2,900-sq.-ft. home seems much larger than its true size, and a full basement, attic, and garage offer plenty of storage and mechanical space.

GETTING IT DONE

Six months was spent in drawing and bidding the project and almost a full year in building the home—relatively efficient given the level of detail and site conditions encountered. A young, energetic builder, Paul Torcellini of Waverly Construction, was selected as general contractor before the structural design and final details were implemented, and his input was directly reflected in the final design. All this coordination kept the design fees relatively low—well below 10 percent of the total construction costs.

Every year, hundreds of thousands of couples become empty-nesters, ultimately retire, and dramatically change their lifestyles. Many move to planned communities that they must adapt to. But a growing number of young retirees demand more personal expression and autonomy. Taking control of your life always involves risk. That risk is minimized by hiring the right people to guide your way through unchartered waters. The rewards are obvious.

KITCHEN CENTRAL. A flue over the cooktop built by the owner dominates the kitchen, basking in the light of skylights and set between the tie rods used to hold walls together.

Hands-On House

FRED KESSLER BUILT STEEL TUGBOATS FOR 20 YEARS.

When he delivered his last steel vessel in 1995, he knew retirement would change his life. He decided that part of the change would be building his own house, and that domestic expression would give life to his chosen profession. Instead of welding huge pieces of steel together to create large-scale structures, he dove into a new way to use his skill as a welder. Fred now creates playful depictions of animals and plants from industrial-strength sheet steel. In time, he also married an interior designer, Arlene, and they decided to literally cement their relationship into the place where they lived.

The Kesslers live in a region where hands-on art is a tradition—near Asheville, North Carolina, the home of Penland, a great crafts school, and before that the legendary Black Mountain College. Fred's shop is located in nearby Mount Pleasant, where, for many years he would cut out a small steel animal for every visitor who stopped by. Even though the nearest neighbor was more than a mile away, he established relationships over the years with a wide variety of people who ended up helping the couple build their new house for an extraordinarily affordable price.

TWO BY TWO. Set in the woods, the owner's depiction of Noah's ark serves as the first welcoming gesture to those driving up to the house. [left]

WATER GARDEN. The concrete steps and cascading water blend beautifully with the plants that thrive in the warm North Carolina environment. [far left]

● ● ● **STUDY WALL.** The study has a smaller overhang than the living room, but the outside wall puts on display the same beams, rafters, steel pipes and ties, and relentlessly right-angled windows and doors used throughout the house.

CRAFT ON THE GRID

Before they could build anything, the Kesslers needed a design. They'd seen a house they loved in a magazine and contacted its architect, Alfredo De Vido, a New York City architect with many years' experience designing small homes on a budget. As you might expect, many of the Kesslers' design inputs were crafts generated (they even had two different craftspeople make their bathroom sinks). They personally created or provided several decorative elements including a cast frieze, a range hood, and an amazing fireplace surround. They also had a very tight budget (initially $80,000, which ultimately grew to $140,000).

To design the house, De Vido used a rigorous right-angle grid (based on a 3-ft. 8-in. by 3-ft. 8-in. module), keeping layout and joinery basic. The modular system of dimensioning clarifies the design of anything—whether it's the size of a room, the width of a planter, or the location of a column.

This modular system was applied to a slab-on-grade building with two bedrooms and a study on its main level, a loft above an elevated entry, and a small basement for mechanical equipment. The house is a linear building set snugly into the south-sloping hillside to open itself up to the sun; its concrete floor holds heat in the winter when the sun is low (see the sidebar on p. 138).

FRONT ENTRY. Flanked by the owner-built trellis, the front door has a wide overhang with steel posts and ties set at the classic 90-degree pitch of the roofs. The entry is at the half level, with a loft above and a lower living space beyond.

VIEW FROM THE ENTRY. Looking out over the top of the fireplace, you can see through to the dining area with the dominant cathedral ceiling leading off to the right and the projecting cathedral ceiling of the living room beckoning beyond. [below]

Craftily Done

THIS SMALL HOUSE IN THE WOODS has a sense of personal expression that can't be duplicated by purchased decoration. The home's unique enrichments include the decorative frieze over the south-facing doors (made by pressing leaves into a plaster mold); bathroom sinks created by local potters; tiles surrounding the fireplace custom-made by a ceramic artist; and steel tiles fabricated by the homeowner. The owners also made the stair rails, railings, trellis, and even the dining-room table. As a finishing touch, once construction was finished, the owners designed and crafted the water garden that surrounds the house and the concrete walkways.

MASTER BEDROOM. This simple space is enriched by art and craft and the interconnection between vaulted ceilings.

A SIMPLE PLAN

The 2,000-sq.-ft. house has an oblong plan that carefully limits the amount of space eaten up by circulation. At the entry stairs, the fireplace and level changes help draw people to the lower level of the vaulted living-room space. The house is conventionally framed, and on the interior its basic structural elements are hidden behind drywall, except where steel tie rods reveal themselves in the vaulted ceilings. On the outside, roofs and eaves have expressed rafters, steel ties, and pipe columns that provide support, create arbors, and allow architecture to fuse with craft.

Although the house is simple in layout, its interior is greatly enriched by the use of cathedral ceilings and Fred's steel work (used both decoratively and structurally). By setting the vaulted interior spaces at right angles to each other, each room is allowed to stake out its own space while keeping the visual flow open throughout the common areas. Additionally, Arlene used color to great effect on interior surfaces, transforming De Vido's design and her husband's craftsmanship into something that is both personalized and softened from its potential edginess.

HELPING HANDS

The Kesslers employed many of their lifelong friends in crafts and construction when creating their home. Aside from hiring two part-time carpenters, all the other trades (electric, plumbing, stucco, HVAC, and drywall) were performed by neighbors who happened to be professionals in the field. The design evolved over time to save money as well. Elaborate trusses were designed down to steel collar ties, wooden or concrete posts became steel tubes, and the fireplace and range hood went from generic models to customized extravaganzas reflective of Mr. Kessler's expertise.

STAIR AND FIREPLACE DETAIL. Native yellow pine blends with handcrafted steel and custom-made tiles to create an interweaving of material, line, plane, and color.

DINING/KITCHEN. Steel columns, collar ties, and flue shroud contrast with the drywalled interior and polished concrete floor. The architectural quality of all these surfaces is balanced by the wide variety of folk art on display throughout the house. [right]

ENTRY ON THE UPHILL SIDE. Gabled projections from this long, thin house draw the eye to the entry. The cascading platforms that control the natural grade were designed and built by the owners themselves, as was the steel trellis, which supports a fledgling climbing vine. [top left]

DINING AREA LOOKING INTO LIVING ROOM. Collar ties, track lighting, window mullions, and a steel column provide multiple rhythms amid this interconnected open space. The transition from concrete floors in the dining area to wood floors in the living room creates a distinction without walls. [top right]

Passive Solar Design

AS MUCH AS ANY HOUSE IN THIS BOOK, this home illustrates the principles of passive solar design that help minimize the cost of heating and cooling. Although the climate of North Carolina is relatively benign during heating times, winter nights can be pretty crisp and, as you might expect, summers can have some fairly heated impact on the interior micro-climate. This home mitigates these extremes with four simple techniques that any homeowner can use in any climate to minimize the costs of heating or cooling:

- Orient the long sides of the house facing south and north. In climates where heat is desired, place glass to face south. In climates where extra heat is to be avoided, the windows' long direction can be faced north.

- Create deep roof overhangs to keep unwanted solar gain out. In this house, tall gable roof extensions are set fully in shade by a 10-ft. overhang off the living room and a 5-ft. overhang at the study.

- Use the floor itself as a "thermal flywheel." The concrete slab floors store heat gain from low-penetrating sunlight in the winter for nighttime radiant heating and effectively take on the temperature of below-grade earth (typically 50°F) when they are left in shade to help offset the seasonally hot air in summer.

- If the site allows it (and this one did), use the natural grade to partially bury the side of your home to either avoid solar heating or, in the case of this house, to allow the earth to provide an extraordinary layer of insulation to the north.

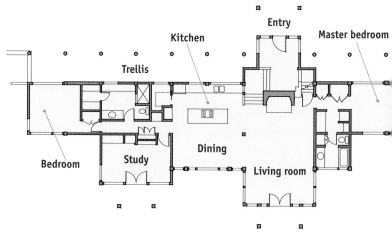

FIRST-FLOOR PLAN

This linear house has its north side dug into a hill. All spaces on the south side have large overhangs to prevent overheating.

Location:	North Carolina
Year Built:	1996
Architect:	Alfredo De Vido
Finished Heated Space:	2,000 sq. ft.
Costs:	Project Budget—$140,000
	Site Development—$10,000
	Design Fee—$10,000

● ● ● **WEST DOWNHILL.** A water garden designed and built by the owners sits in full view of the study (to the right) and the guest bedroom (to the left).

LIVING ROOM. Wraparound standard glazing looks out to a deep overhang through to the woods, while outside and inside are brought together by the small porch. Steel rod collar ties hold walls together and find stylistic resonance with the stock track lighting—both are used to provide a linear counterpart to the expansive drywalled ceilings. [facing page]

BACK COURT. House parts that are unspectacular by themselves—such as doors, windows, transoms, and steps—gain a sense of presence when combined in a confined space.

Courting Favor

WHEN PEOPLE THINK ABOUT BUILDING THEIR OWN HOME,

there are two worlds before them. The first is what they see around them—predictable, artless stereotypes. By doing very little beyond sheltering their occupants, these homes are inherently cheaper to build than custom-built houses. The second stereotype showcases the domestic desires of the rich and famous that are out of touch with anything the average housing consumer could ever afford.

Homeowners who are committed and think clearly can go beyond these two options. Rather than buy a stock-plan stereotype or have your heart broken by out-of-reach fantasies, you can have a house that fits you and your budget.

STARTING OUT HANDS ON

In this spirit, James Mary O'Connor and Sue O'Brien, new arrivals from Ireland, wished to create a harbor for their family. Since they were building in pricey Santa Monica, California, they needed to use every possible method of cost saving to build a home of their own. They had a couple of big advantages. First, they were architects themselves (which not only saves money on the design fee

Use changes of level to create separations between spaces.

ARCHITECTURE TRANSFORMED BY LANDSCAPE. In the years since this southern California house was completed, native plants have transformed the property. Railings-cum-trellises support vigorous growth, softening potentially sharp edges and blurring the distinction between the natural and the man-made. [top]

COURTYARD FROM THE LIVING ROOM. The outdoor terrace and the living room are set at almost the same level, which encourages an easy flow of foot traffic from one to the other. [bottom]

FROM LIVING ROOM INTO STAIRWAY. Cascading steps and recessed openings mark the subtle interplay between parts that are carefully proportioned and clearly set to contrast the placid spaces of this small house. [facing page]

but also affords a knowledge base that few others have). Second, O'Connor and O'Brien acted as their own general contractor; in other words, while they did not actually build the home with their own hands, they hired all the subcontractors and purchased all the materials.

Given that design and construction coordination were in house, this project started with about a 20 percent to 30 percent discount from the retail price tag of a house that is professionally designed and includes a contractor's profit and overhead. But what makes this house so valuable to the vast majority of homeowners who don't have these advantages are the built solutions to typical problems that anyone can use in creating a memorable house on a relatively modest budget.

A SITE FOR SORE EYES

O'Connor and O'Brien found a site in a reasonable location that had an old 18-ft. by 24-ft. garage sitting on the property. They didn't have the funds to remove it, so they left it as is and built up to it. The plan uses this tiny site (no more than ⅛ acre) to the fullest, utilizing a basic "L" shape, which, with the remnant garage, creates an entry court with direct access to the living spaces. There's room for a second rear courtyard as well, and extensive garden planning makes the most of this basic layout. To get the budget under control, generic materials are used without curves,

● ●
●
○

BATHROOM. The simple alignment of tile to win-dowsill and the use of expressive colors make a basic bathroom delightful. [far left]

MASTER BEDROOM. Contrasting colors add spice to the room, while flat stock trim highlights the openings. Dropping the beam at the peak of the roof saves money because rafters can be loosely framed over it rather than tightly miter cut to the beam. [left]

angles, or stylized decoration. Flat stock wood trim, clear and painted, and painted drywall are set to precut 8-ft. and 10-ft. 2x4 walls to create some elegantly simple forms and openings. Standard windows and doors that are thoughtlessly placed by rote into a house form (the rule for the production housing that over-whelms the marketplace) can be the kiss of death if any sense of delight is desired. Here, stock windows and doors are carefully ganged together and strategically located for maximum effect.

SAVINGS WITHIN

The parts of this house that you can't see helped save money as well. Below all the floors is a basic slab-on-grade foundation, which is appropriate for the almost-tropical climate of Santa Monica. One of the inherent problems of a slab-on-grade founda-tion is that it is hard to accommodate mechanical systems under the slab. But in this case, the owners opted to lift two-thirds of the house's floor three steps up on wood platform framing to allow mechanical equipment to be fed through a simple horizontal chase. This had the additional benefit of allowing the sunken living room's concrete floor to be set virtually at grade, providing easy access to the front and back courtyards.

Drywall is the rule of the day for all interior walls and ceilings. However, it was Sue O'Brien's sense of color, inspired by colorist Tina Beebe, that allowed this blandest of materials to come to life.

● ○ ● **DIAGONAL VIEW.** Interior views across this open floor plan create a sense of scale and space that belies the house's modest size. Wood, color, and drywall act in concert with the artwork and lighting to create a space that is both lively and controlled.

HOME OFFICE. Set beyond a gauntlet of bookcases, a seemingly distant office bathed in light from a shed dormer is in fact only a few steps away from the master bedroom.

Drywall Dramatics

WHEN YOUR BUDGET IS TIGHT, your palette of materials usually shrinks, but that doesn't mean there's less room for artistic expression. One way to bring life to standard drywall is to paint blank walls different colors, but it was not enough in this case. In and around the staircase and fireplace, O'Connor and O'Brien opted to add "layers" of applied walls that are gapped to create shadow lines and voids, all reinforced with judicious application of color. These three-dimensional shapes create relatively large-scale elements in a small house and provide the sort of inexpensive kinetic touches that transform mundane materials into unique objects.

Local focal points give simple spaces purpose.

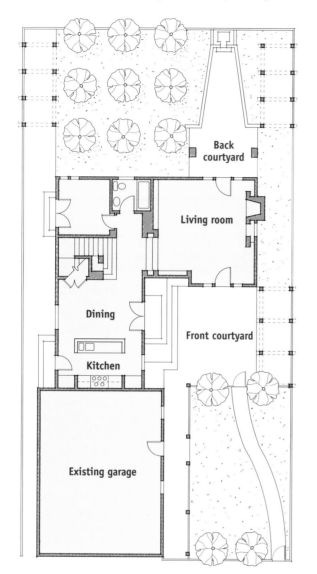

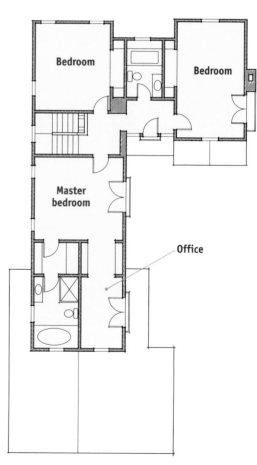

FIRST-FLOOR PLAN

Set on a tiny lot, an L-shaped house attached to an existing old garage is set back from the street, creating a delightful courtyard.

SECOND-FLOOR PLAN

The long leg of the "L" serves as a master suite/home office partially built over the existing garage.

Location:	**Santa Monica, California**
Year Built:	1996
Architect:	James Mary O'Connor
Finished Heated Space:	1,850 sq. ft.
Costs:	Project Budget—$200,000
	Site Development—$8,000
	Design Fee—owner/architect

architect James Mary O'Connor

"We were influenced in our color choice by colorist Tina Beebe and Mexican architect Luis Barragan, and more globally by an infusion of visual inspiration from California, Mexico, and Japan. Late at night the colors glow like an illuminated box of jewels."

There are perhaps 20 different shades of color used throughout the house, some subtle and some bold. Beyond simply painting walls different colors, drywall was also used to shroud overtly sculptural shapes and freestanding pieces of framed wall layered onto the fireplace, the stairs, and other surfaces (see the sidebar on p. 145). These elements also have a functional role, helping to create avenues for mechanical lines (the laundry is tucked away below the stair build-out as well).

A TIGHT WEAVE OF SPACE

All of these cost-saving elements were important, but the key to making this house affordable was the downsizing of the building to make it maximally efficient. Virtually the entire house is two-story (doubling up the efficiency of the foundation), and O'Connor and O'Brien managed to create a four-bedroom, three-bath house in all of 1,850 sq. ft.—not counting the garage's existing 400 sq. ft. Rather than create a rabbit warren of tiny spaces to obtain this small size, this house has a calm openness that reflects the designers' other inspiration, architect Luis Barragan, along with an affinity for the sensibilities of indigenous Mexican and Japanese architecture.

Spatial magic was achieved in three simple ways. First, spaces are directly linked and flow together through what architects like to call an open floor plan. Second, there is the gift of height: 10-ft. ceilings for the living room and lightly vaulted ceilings for almost every space on the second floor help defeat the sense of compression that might have resulted from the oppressive 8-ft.

● ● ● **STAIRS/DINING.** By adding layers of drywall to create both voids and thicker wall elements, and painting those elements in marvelously interactive colors, the simplest tools of construction are turned into sculpture. The laundry is efficiently concealed behind the double doors of the drywall box. [facing page]

DINING ROOM. Directly connected to the outdoors and the living room, the higher-than-normal ceilings and larger-than-normal openings allow a tight space to become light-filled and decompressed. [above]

KITCHEN AND DINING. Simple stock cabinets framed with painted drywall bathe in the glow of outsized windows to create a wonderful sense of material, light, and space for remarkably little money.

●●● **FROM ENTRY INTO LIVING ROOM.** Relatively tall ceiling heights and larger-than-expected openings stand in contrast to the tight floor plan, while the resonant color of the hearth is a focal point that draws us into the home.

FIREPLACE. Creating mass and void with color and light, shape and space, all is fashioned with the simplest of standard materials. Color is the crucial element in fusing a stock firebox, a window, and wall materials into something between sculpture and architecture. [facing page]

ceiling heights that are standard in most houses today. Third, outdoor space is used extensively for social activities. In this case, not only was the house layout designed to make outdoor rooms, but O'Connor and O'Brien created large-scale overhangs, trellises, and carefully located plantings that allow the outdoors to become a natural extension of the built parts of the home.

In their own sometimes-obscure lingo, architects talk about transparency (the intimate interweaving of aligned spaces) and of design based on a tartan grid (the consistent organization of framing bays to make spaces and shapes). But in this architects' home, the sensibility is one of calm informality rather than abstract aesthetics because the design elements are scaled for human occupancy, not academic theorizing. This simplicity of design is reflected in exterior detailing as well. Stucco is used throughout the exterior; trim is flat stock either painted white or left natural. Modest eaves have open rafter tails to contrast the stucco wall's opacity.

In homes, the proof is in the living. After more than a few years of occupancy, the owners have found this home fully adapted to their lifestyle. Even if you're not an architect and have neither the time nor the energy to become your own general contractor, you may be able to build your own home inexpensively if you use what the world of standardized construction gives you. When popular culture preaches bigger is better and offers up elaboration where simplicity is best, have the courage of James Mary O'Connor and Sue O'Brien, and your dreams will get built.

cost-effective.

DECK AT DUSK. Multiple cantilevers create a structural sculpture set in nature, with basic framing components brought to life by the careful detailing and angled projection. Subtle changes of color are used to differentiate between the green skin of the house and the subordinate gray painted deck.

Art in the Woods

WHEN ARTHUR ROGER AND SCOTT BEARD DECIDED THAT THEY HAD TO FIND relief from their high-pressure lifestyle operating one of New Orleans's most in-demand art galleries, they opted for a seemingly unglamorous solution. Rather than seek out some trendy beach locale or society enclave, they chose Poplarville, Mississippi, which was a drivable distance from work. Similarly, when they decided to build their own home, they rejected building a "statement" house that would sit proudly on some manicured lawn, coastline, or hill-top. Instead, their house virtually slinks into the near-tropical woods of the deep South. The unpretentious site on the Wolf River, chosen because of its kayak-friendly navigability and its raw sensibility, was dubbed the "Snake Ravine" by the owners after their most immediate neighbors.

A HOUSE IN PARTS

With a clear vision of what their domestic getaway was *not* to be, Beard and Roger opted to go with an architecture firm they'd worked with before on their gallery. The irony of having a firm named Urban Instruments (led by principal Wellington Reiter) design a house in the deep woods of Mississippi is not lost on the

● ● ● **THE PATH TO THE HOUSE.** With trees giving way to columns and green siding, the red clay soil leading to red stained decking, and the canopy of trees replicating the roof overhead, the built world subtly imposes itself on the world of natural light and botanic growth. [photos this page]

BAY SPACE. Perfect for a home owned by art gallery owners, this entire extended bay is filled from corner to corner with a favorite painting, making a room out of a minor extension. The bay is further defined at its outside edges by two fir columns. [facing page]

ambience of the house itself. Rather than an updated bucolic vision of a Southern home, what now inhabits these woods is a sleek, linear counterpoint to the virgin forest, held above the occasionally overflowing river on 20 concrete piers.

This is a house whose detailing respects its limited budget and the surrounding woods. With spaces more akin to the owners' art gallery than their full-time residence (an in-town traditional townhouse), the house is formed by three separate pieces connected by ramps, walkways, balconies, and porches. The home has a sinuous quality that belies its true 1,800-sq.-ft. size, and because of all the interconnecting extensions, there is well over 800 sq. ft. of usable outdoor space.

This shady idyll has four tightly designed bedrooms and two-and-a-half baths, making the most of the available budget while practicing "stealth technology" in architectural form. When dealing with sites that have an overwhelming character, architects often use extreme contrast to express themselves (such as Frank Lloyd Wright's Guggenheim Museum set in the flat wall of Fifth Avenue building facades or Philip Johnson's crystalline Glass House in the rolling Connecticut landscape). In this house, painted

Don't fight the site—fitting in (or in between) almost always saves money.

Stock Sculpture

AS MUCH AS ANY PROJECT IN THIS BOOK, this home uses standard materials to make virtual sculptures out of trellises, stairs, railings, and other structurally expressive elements. Stock lumber comes in simple rectangular cross sections, but here, one side of these plain 2x's is cut to a curve. These lightly sculpted sticks are rhythmically oriented and combined to form structure, shading devices, and railings with exposed steel fasteners to turn generic building materials into sculptural events—an appropriate ambience for owners who run an art gallery.

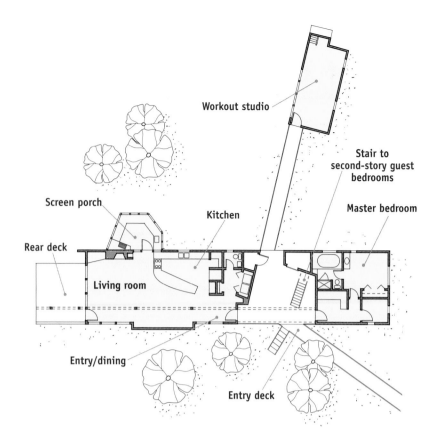

Workout studio

Stair to
second-story guest
bedrooms

Screen porch

Kitchen

Master bedroom

Rear deck

Living room

Entry/dining

Entry deck

Location:	**Poplarville, Mississippi**
Year Built:	1997
Architect:	Wellington Reiter, Urban Instruments
Finished Heated Space:	1,800 sq. ft.
Costs:	Project Budget—$250,000±
	Design Fee—withheld

SITE/FLOOR PLAN

A central entry deck separates the sleeping and living
spaces, with a small gymnasium accessed by a secondary
bridge to the north.

plywood siding and gray metal roof serve as blank backdrops to
the animated treescape. Rather than boldly confront its surroundings, the subtle exterior of this house will continue to
recede visually as the trees mature.

The elongated home has projections for a screen porch, decks,
and a bumped-out art niche. Its 19-ft.-wide by 88-ft.-long shape also
casts off another little building into the woods—one so intimately
related to its environment that its location was left to be determined
in the field as the house was being built. This 12-ft. by 20-ft. "mini-
me" to the house has its own deck, separately accessed second floor,
and elevated walkway. It serves as a gymnasium and guest room.

ART INSIDE AND OUT

The house has a clear functional layout. The service spaces
(baths, laundry, kitchen, and storage) huddle toward a central
open deck-cum-court at the end of the long walkway that provides entry to the elevated house. This layout allows the other
living spaces to have at least three sides open to light and air. The
open deck, which is scooped out of the overall bar shape of the
building, is a virtual town square tying together the various parts
of the house. Contrasting with this entry court is an odd-shaped
screen porch, an obvious extension, which projects beyond the

● ○ ● **ENTRY DECK INTO MASTER BEDROOM.** In a house of multiple
focal points and angles, the master bedroom door is framed
by the bridge (right) and the stair to the guest bedrooms
(left), with a canopy of exposed rafters and plywood sheathing
overhead. [above]

SPINE LINE. With only a thin line of structure of timber and
steel running the length of the house, the dining room
(left) and living room (right) lay out freely in this sea of
space and light. [facing page]

MASTER BEDROOM ENTRY. A wall of built-ins in the
master bedroom, which follows the line of the spine
of columns, provides a density of storage not found
in most closets. Beyond the bedroom door, the view
leads across the entry court to the living room.

KITCHEN. Stained wood, color, and high-tech furnishings
and appliances give this active space a bistro feel. [top,
facing page]

WORKOUT STUDIO. Set behind the rear entry deck, the bridge
to the workout shed launches from a flat wall of stained
clapboards. The second floor accommodates a guest bedroom loft. [bottom, facing page]

living space into the landscape. In addition, the house extends
upward to create two separate guest bedroom suites. The master
bedroom below is separated from the living space by the outdoor
court itself.

The home's interior opens directly out to the woods. At the
end of the living room, a wall of glass creates an interior viewing
platform: It's as though these gallery owners have put their
whole site on exhibit. Interior surfaces are standard fare, but they
gain luster through crisp detailing and surface treatment. Clear-
finished pine floors and composite wood panels, yellow pine
ceilings, a faux stone tile fireplace front, deeply stained wood
cabinets, and a series of warm and cool painted tones make this
a rich ensemble of surface, shape, and light. Structure is exposed
at the home's central spine, made up of a row of columns and a
continuous beam of large fir timbers (occasionally reinforced by
steel wire and struts).

This is the sort of informal architecture that can allow electric
fans to be lag-bolted to the wall, a prefabricated firebox to show
off its galvanized steel flue, and stairs and railings to be fashioned
with raw materials. Larger elements like the kitchen and the artwork itself take full advantage of the open space and generous
ceiling height.

FRESH AND COMFORTABLE

The best houses are often formed by the dance between familiarity
and the unexpected: a brick townhouse has a red door, a tiny
Cape has a huge window facing a great view, or a home on a

Minimize the number of internal supports; one central support is always cheaper to build.

● ● ● **FIREPLACE, WITH PORCH BEYOND.** A standard firebox is dressed up with a beveled surround clad in simulated slate. The brightly painted sculptural built-ins and drywall around the firebox, the exposed metal flue, and the clerestory windows above provide a rich contrast to the deep, cool tones of the screen porch beyond.

LIVING ROOM END. The expanse of glass, the openness of the railing (which uses stayed cables as the barrier), and the simple harmonies of aligned structure provide a transparent transition from living room to cantilevered deck to the Mississippi woods. [left]

dark site is filled with light from skylights. Here, the familiarity between the owners, the architect, and their native climate resulted in a house that blankly accommodates the wooded site while its interior explodes with space and life.

People often feel there are two basic choices when you build a home. Either you go with the flow, accept the cards you're dealt, and make the context and budget your friends, or you beat against the tide and try to make a square peg fit in a round hole, either stylistically or budgetarily. Here, budget and art work together to form a home that reflects the owners' sensibilities to a T, while at the same time paying quiet deference to its subtly beautiful wild surroundings.

FACING SOUTH. With the shed extension of the main house to the left and the detached studio to the right, the stark, grounded forms blend into the landscape.

Big Sky Trio

AFTER LIVING IN AN IN-TOWN HOME WITH A HOUSE-BOUND OFFICE, photographer Audrey Hall decided she wanted to change the way she lived and worked. Moving to the wilds of Montana, Audrey opted to create a small ensemble of buildings that would separate where she worked from where she lived. Anything man-made would stand in stark counterpoint to the dynamic world of Big Sky country, with its open horizons and distant mountains, and while it would have been easy (and all too predictable) to build a faux folk art homage to the agrarian west, Audrey wanted something more.

Even though she had a clear vision of what she wanted, she knew that the built answer to her domestic needs was not an easy one, so she looked for professional help. In talking to architects Lori C. Ryker and Brett W. Nave, principals of Ryker/Nave Design, Audrey found kindred spirits, and even though her limited budget would have to include the architects' fee of 7 percent of construction costs, the results speak for themselves. Ryker/Nave did what all good designers do: They took the gist of their client's dream of domesticity and made a design that does not pander to pat pre-conceptions. This is neither a faux ranch nor a transplanted ranch

Basic materials are anything but when they're organized by an artful eye.

house, but rather a unique set of buildings that reflect the realities of the site, the client, and the budget.

LAYOUT IN THE OUTLANDS

The three buildings, which provide separate structures for work, cars, and living, stake out their turf on a circular one-acre lot in a sea of open space. The two outbuildings (garage and studio) are set at an angle to the main house, which orients its double-height living space to accept the low winter sun and collect heat in its concrete slab floor. Not unlike a house on the water where the water view is "the front," here the sweeping southerly view of the surrounding mountains naturally orients the house away from the road on the north side.

The main house harbors a virtually independent first-floor guest living space with two bedrooms and a bath. This guest wing borders the totally open living/dining area, with the common areas of the house set within an exposed timber frame. This timber structure combines the front door and stair to form an entry with a Big Sky view straight through a two-story slot of space. Half of the second floor of the main living space is a master suite, with a bathroom directly over the kitchen; the other half is given over to the double-height space for the stair and living area below.

While the residence (by far the largest part of this 2,600-sq.-ft. ensemble) has a variety of subtle and dramatic elaborations upon

FACING EAST. The trio of buildings (house left, garage center, studio right) is carefully laid out in an open meadow with rolling hills behind, all set within the grand sweep of Big Sky country. [top]

MAIN ENTRY. The three forms of gable, shed, and stoop roof all come together at the point of entry, while the garage (right) helps create a courtyard that frames the façade, enabling the necessary scale change from "Big Sky" to "home." [above]

KITCHEN AND DINING. The furniture mimics the stark simplicity of the home's structure, which is all on display. Natural light highlights the two-part harmony between wood surfaces and white walls. [facing page]

Shadow Play

IN CREATING THIS TRIO OF BUILDINGS, Ryker/Nave Design used basic materials to create simple shapes that both catch light and, more distinctively, provide shadow. Cutting one eave line of the dominant gable roof form at a slightly rakish angle (rather than paralleling the wall that is below it) protects the wall from sun and rain but also displays a human touch. By recessing one corner of the gable roof, providing large overhangs for all the buildings, and mounting the 2x4 framing of the garage on the outside of the walls, an ever-changing world of shadow and plane is created in this land of crisp sunlight.

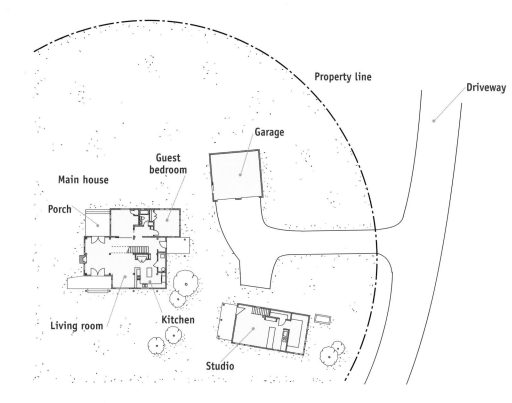

Property line

Driveway

Garage

Guest
bedroom

Main house

Porch

Living room

Kitchen

Studio

SITE FLOOR PLAN

Two oblong boxes (the garage and studio) flank the front-door side of the home. The "true" front faces south and opens out to the dramatic views of the mountains beyond.

the classic wood architecture of the Wild West, the garage and the studio are simple buildings fashioned of stark shapes and materials—with a couple of tweaks. Most of the roofs are straightforward gables or sheds, but one eave is cut at an angle, and the shed roof that covers the guest bedroom wing is extended beyond the side of its parent building, creating a corner for the detached rooflet at the entry to nestle into. One corner of the main house is carefully recessed to form a covered porch facing the southerly view and the morning sun. The main building combines stick framing and a post-and-beam cage of wood supporting the main portion of the house. This grid of wood is literally "slipped" so that the home's walls are held away from the timber frame (see the sidebar on p. 166).

The trio of buildings have some common themes. All roofing is sheet metal, all exterior siding is local wood left natural (and often knotty), and all interior structure is exposed. The stairs are a simple straight run, and all ground-level floors are poured concrete slab on grade. Similarly, windows are all standard units, though they are arranged in a variety of ways, from random to ganged to centered.

It is in the sophisticated reinterpretation of everyday materials and techniques that designs such as this find a spark of life. A

Location:	Livingston, Montana
Year Built:	2002
Architect:	Ryker/Nave Design
Finished Heated Space:	1,850 sq. ft. (house), 750 sq. ft. (studio)
Costs:	Project Budget—$285,000
	Site Development—$13,000
	Design Fee—$20,000

● ● ● **FIREPLACE WINDOW WALL.** Big planes of glass and a simple, isolated fireplace are both framed and surrounded by the timber structure, while the concrete floor is polished to give a real sense of grounded texture.

Separated by Design

THIS HOUSE HAS A UNIQUE APPROACH to post-and-beam framing, using a structural skeleton to support stick-frame walls and roof. Normally, post-and-beam structures utilize "SIPS" panels—a sandwich of plywood or flakeboard outside surfaces with a solid injected-foam core—that are directly mounted to the outside of a cage of timbers. The SIPS system prevents condensation problems that occur when you stick-frame between the post-and-beam frame as there is no way to provide a vapor barrier without hiding the post-and-beam structure. In this house, the stick-built walls do not sit between the openings of the frame but are set away from it, either outside or inside the grid of posts and beams. Not only does this leave the structure exposed, but it's also cheaper to stick-frame a skin rather than use SIPS panels.

panel slides to be both a wall and a door separating the shed wing from the main body of the house. The partition for the lofty second-floor master bedroom is a virtual adaptation of corn-crib architecture (wood slats with cut openings complete with rotating shutters). By taking wood and basic joinery techniques and letting them be tweaked in full view turns predictable into poignant.

KEEPING THE ART AFFORDABLE

The house was built for just over $100 per square foot, which for a home of this carefully intricate and quirky design is inexpensive even in Montana. Using off-the-shelf materials and a layout devoid of angles and curves helped keep costs down, as did the fact that Audrey installed the insulation and radiant-floor heating herself and did all of the painting and staining in the house.

The dual role of Ryker/Nave as designer *and* builder also helped to control costs. The norm is to have a separate builder and architect who look over each other's shoulders and play off each other. In this case, Ryker/Nave followed the owner's basic specs for everything, but fine-tuned those material desires as necessary throughout the design and building of the project. A side benefit of this dual role was that construction started three months after the design was initiated, as all bidding was in-house

● ○ ○ **VIEW FROM THE PORCH.** French doors open wide to reveal the majesty of the distant mountains.

STUDIO PORCH. Facing south, this spare overhang has a deep cantilever above and bare-bones columns below. Used as temporary full-time housing while the main house was being built, this tiny structure sat dwarfed by the mountains, sky, and prairie that surround it. [facing page]

homeowner Audrey Hall

"The design and building process has been a continual dialogue between the architect/ builders and me. Philosophical discussions about environmentally responsible design, brainstorming ideas about making the project affordable, conversations about 'cookie-cutter architecture,' and a prominent awareness of fixtures and materials have all been at the forefront of the entire project. Through our discussions, I've discovered that unique, intriguing, and beautiful ideas stem from a shared vision and collaborative efforts."

and most of the detailing was done during construction, telescoping the time it usually takes to design such a carefully crafted building.

BUILDING IN PHASES

Another element that helped make this project affordable is relatively unique compared with the other examples in this book. Building three separate structures allowed for an easy construction schedule as the studio/cottage was built first and served as the temporary residence (and workplace) of the owner, thus allowing the construction of the main building to occur without a killer deadline. In almost every circumstance, the more time available for construction, the less money is spent, as haste literally makes waste when building a home. Taking the time to fine-tune specifications and reality-check on-paper designs with preferences revealed on-site prevents the sort of changes during construction that usually cost dearly. A side benefit was that the joy of construction could be viewed up close and personal by Audrey without having to live in a construction site during the messy, complicated, and often brutally informal exercise of building.

Audrey left her town-bound Victorian house and tiny bedroom office to find a new future in this wild country. Without the thoughtful collaboration between herself and Ryker/Nave Design she might simply have opted for a larger version of what she left behind. This is the typical result when stock plans are applied to a unique life. In taking the risk of partnership with her designer/ builders to create her most prominent (and intimate) possession, Audrey found her way home.

● ● ● **SHELF SCREEN.** The shelving unit bridges the gap between the rough-hewn timber-frame structure and the slab stair, partially screening the living room from the hallway.

BEDROOM IN A BOX. Overtly agrarian in its origins, gapped wood sheathing combines with thick flooring in the master bedroom suite to create a building within a building. Raw steel railings and structural fittings counterpoint this wood sculpture. [left]

OPENINGS IN THE WALL. Patterned after corn-crib construction, pivoting wall panels and gapped boards reveal the wonderful contrast between sapwood and heartwood. [below left]

STAIRWAY TO BEDROOM. The open stair and its metal railing artfully combine with the built-in bookcases, which are constructed of the exact same materials, lending a sense of lightness and sprightly ascendance to the second-floor master bedroom suite. [below]

LIVING ROOM INTO KITCHEN. The living room drops down three steps from the first-floor level and soars upward to the full height of the butterfly roof. Within this well-composed space, painted surfaces contrast with the wood tones of the interior, including the sitting stoop in the foreground.

Freestyle

WHEN YOU FINALLY MAKE THE DECISION TO BUILD YOUR OWN HOME, the rush of empowerment soon gives way to the fear of bankruptcy. It may come as a shock to learn that slavishly adhering to a specific house style (colonial, Arts and Crafts, Shingle style, or even contemporary) can force your hand in ways that are inherently expensive. When style imposes nonnegotiable specs for materials and the basic shape of the building, the net result may have no benefit beyond being "correct." Simplicity may trump style when you contemplate the cost of your home.

When budget is paramount, economics can create its own sense of style. Richard Shugar, an architect from Eugene, Oregon, fully understood the hidden costs of style. When he thought of building his own home, he and his wife Kamala were young and without children, and he was starting his own business. Like many first-time home buyers, the Shugars were looking to a future that probably included children and an income stream that would inevitably have its ups and downs, so it took no small amount of courage to build a house. Based on so many unknowns, it is remarkable that such a confident and expressive house springs out of a ⅕-acre lot surrounded by three streets in suburban Eugene.

 TWO SHAPES, ONE PRESENCE. On a tight suburban lot, two boxes with butterfly roofs, projecting bays, bold colors, and natural materials make an undeniable impact amid the existing mature trees. The natural location for the entry is between these two boxes (center) where the site is relatively flat. [above right]

SIDING. Board-and-batten siding wraps the entry floor of the house, while the corrugated metal bay (right) extends second-floor bedrooms. The wood-shingled second floor adds another layer to the mix. [above]

STEEP LIMITS

Plenty of limits faced the Shugars when they thought about building their home on this tight site. Beyond the lot size, the site also had a dramatic drop in level of almost 30 ft. over the 100 ft. of its length. But as with many small suburban sites near major cities, there was city water and sewer, so some site costs were minimized. If the design left the landscape intact, the owners could focus their money and attention on what was built versus what was put into the ground. This landscape included eleven mature trees that the owners desperately wanted to keep.

The bones of the house are simple. Its shape is formed by two basic boxes that are skewed at a slight angle to each other (allowing three of the trees to be saved) and a deck between the boxes that basks in the mountain view. These boxes burst out of the landscape as the ground falls away on the back side, making the most of the dynamic potential of the hillside site. Rather than shyly sidling down the slope, this house uses a raking roofline formed by "butterfly" roofs (see the sidebar on p. 175) to actively engage the landscape.

When you have a sloping site, you can either dig into a hillside or let the hillside run under your house. In this case, the architect did both. Where he needed to (at the garage) and where there was the least amount of slope to deal with, he used

DINING INTO LIVING ROOM. Open stairs and framing and large windows create a sea of light made more dramatic by the use of bold colors and natural materials. The balcony off the central stair platform (just visible at center) is suspended by a steel rod from the lowest point of the butterfly roof above. [above]

SENSITIVE SITING. The house was oriented to respect the existing mature trees on the site. Here, with steps and house to one side and deck to the other, there's an undeniable sense of integrating the house and the landscape. [left]

● ●● **LAYERED VIEWS.** With second-floor openings aligned between the two main boxes and the entry, and the height provided by the butterfly roof, the house expands visually.

compacted fill to provide space for a car to sit within the envelope of the house. Where the slope was steepest, he simply spanned over it and created a partial basement where the slope was at its lowest and required the least excavation. Crawl spaces were used everywhere else.

INSIDE UP

Inside, the upwardly angled butterfly roofs serve to expand the home's sense of space, not only in the second-floor rooms directly below the roof, but also in the double-height living room. Within this living area, a cantilevered stair landing projects into the open space, its walls painted a bold violet. Shugar created a classic open plan on the first floor, complete with a step-down lower-level living area. The central 24-ft. by 14-ft. deck expands the view upon entry to the house and allows the living space to virtually double in size during fair weather. Shugar also opened up the entire second-floor area by aligning doorways to interconnect the two boxes.

Because of the open plan, there is almost no space dedicated purely to circulation in this house, except for the staircase and the entry. An office is used as the connector on the second floor between the two boxes. A loft play space connects the two children's sleeping spaces on the second floor above the kitchen.

e flexibility to choose what fits your budget.

● ● ● **DOWNHILL.** Viewed from the back side, a third level is revealed—a concrete-block base set below the middling red band of painted siding. Projections and connections are also color coded, and the entire form is angled to respect the locations of the existing trees. [right, facing page]

DECK VIEW. The mature trees that were saved help frame the view from the deck, which is protected by the wings of the house and visually enhanced by the open-wire deck rails. [below]

Butterfly Roofs

A BUTTERFLY ROOF IS TRULY AN INVERSION. Rather than having the high point of the roof in the middle (a traditional gable) or at one side (a shed or saw-tooth roof), a butterfly roof turns a gable roof upside down and makes the center the low point. In this house, the architect pushes roof pitches around, making one of the "wings" longer than the other and thus higher.

This type of roof needs a low beam at the center, which usually cuts down on meaningful attic space. On the plus side, a butterfly roof offers a great opportunity to capture light at the perimeter of a building and draw it down into its center and to provide wide open opportunities for natural ventilation. It's also easy to frame.

In the Words of ● ● ●

homeowner Kamala Shugar

"From the beginning, Richard and I worked together to create a home that would be tailored to our lives, and we found ourselves reworking and rethinking various aspects of the design along the way. In the end, the house is a blend of old and new: traditional images that I prefer, like the interior window trim and molding, combined with modern materials that Richard likes. All of these aspects are modified to allow for an open floor plan that allows us to live our lives in a less formal, more farmhouse type of way."

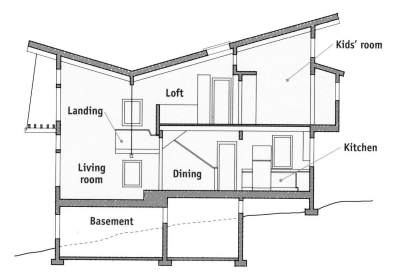

SECTION

A classic butterfly roof allows full clerestory lighting in the children's bedrooms and double-height ceiling space in the living room.

FIRST-FLOOR PLAN

The entry and the splayed-out deck form the link between the smaller garage box and the main box to the north, which is completely open with kitchen-facing street views and a sunken double-height living room looking out toward dramatic views to the west.

Location:	Eugene, Oregon
Year Built:	2001
Architect:	Richard J. Shugar
Finished Heated Space:	1,964 sq. ft.
Costs:	Project Budget—$265,140
	Site Development—none
	Design Fee—$25,000 (retail value)

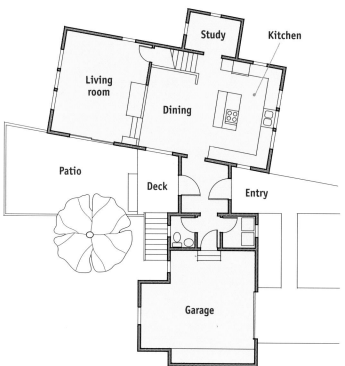

To create all this openness, storage spaces are carefully packed along the outside walls, and bathrooms are sized to take up minimal space. Shugar used double pocket doors to connect the two small children's bedrooms within the 18-ft. width of the larger box and further relieved the potential sense of crowding by setting the loft space directly off these two spaces. An outdoor balcony off the loft space and master bedroom directly expands those spaces into the great outdoors.

MAKING CHOICES

This is not a house without some compromises. The garage is only one-car, the laundry room is tight, the master bath has only one sink, and the study space off the kitchen is a very snug 6 ft. by 9 ft. But Shugar compensated for these economizing gestures with some zesty detailing and spatial drama. Rather than subject this expressive house to the minimal materials of Modernism, he used wood shingles, inexpensive board-and-batten siding with plywood as the "boards," and industrial corrugated sheet-metal siding for projecting bays. In addition, 4-ft.-wide eaves, wood trellises, and those steel-clad bays provide shading and visual kick. At the front door, a rain chain directs water away from the entry. Garage doors are attractively detailed, and the undersides of all the eaves are open-framed. Inexpensive split-faced concrete block provides the base that all this activity rests upon.

KITCHEN/DINING. Set amid open framing and simple wood cabinets, the center-island kitchen is filled with light from the windows centered at the end of the space. The painted trim contrasts with clear-finished natural wood sashes, windowsills, and baseboard detailing, while laminated wood beams find their visual counterpart in the inexpensive short-pieced wood flooring that floods this space.

STRUCTURE ON SHOW. As befits a house for an architect, much of the supporting structure is put on display and uses steel strapping to interconnect exposed laminated wood beams, rafters, and joists.

Stock Material Savings

MANY OF THE HOMES FEATURED IN THIS BOOK use stock material as a way to save money, but this house offers some specifics that may prove helpful:

- The owner (an architect) wanted high-quality windows but could not afford a national line's "architect" series. Instead, he chose a line specifically oriented to builders that had far fewer size options. This ended up saving $6,000.
- Rather than use natural wood trim on the interior, the owner substituted MDF (medium-density fiberboard) sheet stock sawn to the appropriate widths. Although slightly more susceptible to impact damage and moisture absorption, this is a much less expensive material and does not expand and contract as any natural wood product would.
- The flooring was a prefinished engineered product, which saved $2,500 over a standard maple equivalent.
- Carpet was purchased as remnants (in this case, at $5.00 a yard versus $36.00 a yard.)

The interior surfaces rigorously adhere to a limited menu of materials with color used as a counterpoint to the myriad wood elements. There are also more built-ins than the modest budget of $135 per square foot might predictably have allowed.

Unlike many late-20th-century homes, this project is an energy-conscious design. The deep roof overhangs provide shade to prevent overheating, while windows are laid out for solar gain from the south to the double-height living space. Trellises and the mature trees that were saved also help prevent overheating. The roof form and transom windows are oriented to allow natural venting. Ultimately, it is the efficiency of its compact size that enables this three-bedroom, two-and-a-half-bath house to use less energy than its less thoughtfully designed contemporaries.

If rational thought dominated every move, then couples like the Shugars would probably not build such a "risky" house at this early point in their lives. Then again, that same sense of adventure has helped launch Richard Shugar's career—the house has been celebrated in the local press and is a virtual calling card in the materials that he uses to sell his wares to potential clients. Beyond shelter, our homes reflect where our values lie. A young architect aches to express his creativity, a family yearns for a nest. For those who build their home to reflect who they are, dreams really do come true.

● ● ● **LIVING ROOM WINDOWS.** Large standard windows are combined with the open-frame structure to bring light into the double-height living room. The deep overhang overhead provides shade from the high summer sun to prevent overheating.

ENTRY. Framed by corrugated steel and a trellis of painted dimensional lumber that supports a plastic skylight, the natural-finish wood door is the centerpiece of this material medley. The chain to the left guides rainwater off the skylight's edge. [facing page]

SCREEN PORCH INTERIOR. Six pieces of decorative trim applied to the gable end add a touch of whimsy to the simplest of wood-frame structures.

View to the Future

WITH ONE CHILD IN COLLEGE AND ANOTHER WELL INTO HER
high school years, the owners of a renovated 3,500-sq.-ft. colonial house in Connecticut had the good sense to realize that they had two choices: They could either stay put and live in a house that was oversized for their impending change in lifestyle, or they could seize the opportunity to strike out on a new course. Fortunately, they had anticipated these new circumstances and had purchased a one-acre building lot in their neighborhood 10 years earlier.

NEW IN HISTORY

The site they chose had some extraordinary history to it, with a number of ancient foundations dating back to the mid-1600s, and some exceptional natural features, including a small river that ran across the back of the lot and several fully mature trees. The house could capture great views up, down, and across the river, but it needed to avoid the archaeological remains and towering trees as well as fit into the context of a classic New England street. The house also needed to accommodate a master bedroom on the first floor—a virtual requirement for many empty nesters for a long-term occupancy geared for easy living—and allow for a future garage/barn.

The house is a true blend of surprise and comfort.

WRAPAROUND HOUSE. The casual, wraparound quality of the back side of the house, seen from the sitting area the owners created at the river's edge, is given a sense of order through the consistent use of white cedar shingles, green painted window and door sashes, and aligned eaves. [right]

NORTH END. As the roofline steps up, the screen porch steps out, with its applied decorative pieces of cedar reflecting the home's context amid the trees.

Location:	**Madison, Connecticut**
Year Built:	2001
Architect:	Duo Dickinson
Finished Heated Space:	2,325 sq. ft.
Costs:	Project Budget—$365,000
	Site Development—$21,000
	Design Fee—$22,750

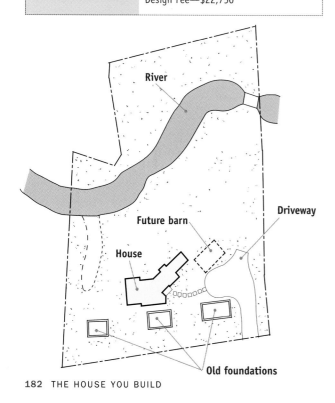

The owners' budget was about $150 per square foot, which, relative to the time and place, presented quite a challenge. The owners looked to contain costs by researching millwork, windows, the heating system, and tile and bath fixtures; compiling extensive lists; drawing sketches; and clipping magazine images. This wealth of preliminary data and their quick and precise feedback as the design was developed helped reduce the architect's fee to less than 7 percent of the project cost. Additionally, they stepped in and fabricated the hundreds of aluminum clips for the radiant heat system.

THE PARTS BUILD A HOUSE

The exceptional site and the owners' input came together in the creation of a unique ensemble of spaces that in turn spawned an active shape. The budget dictated that standard surfaces were used to clad this animated building. Inside, drywall seamlessly wraps an array of interior shapes, while on the outside asphalt roof shingles and unfinished white cedar shingle siding adapt to a wide variety of angled and projecting planes with a minimum of detailing effort.

The house's structure is created almost exclusively from truss joists and dimensional lumber using precisely the same construction techniques as in hundreds of thousands of spec-built homes across the United States. What makes this building special is the

SITTING AREA. As light cascades down from the clerestory windows and skylights above, the cathedral ceiling over the sitting space with the kitchen beyond creates variety of scale, light, and shape unified by the consistent use of trim, drywall, and windows.

One dramatic ornamental gesture can completely reinvent the generic.

Customized with Care

TO BREAK UP THE EXPANSE OF CEDAR SHINGLE SIDING and asphalt shingle roof, this house uses trim at two critical focal points on the exterior: at the column set below the central tower at the corner of the entry portico and at the gabled end wall of the screen porch. Making curvy shapes out of wood is inherently more expensive than using straight shapes, but here the costs were contained in three simple ways.

- First, the column was formed using medium-density overlay, paper-skinned plywood that is normally used by sign makers. Simple bandsawn shapes were cut and spaced using dimensional lumber and plywood to form the three-dimensional "tree" column.

- Second, the applied end pieces of the screen porch gable were sized to fit the overall width of a ¾-in. by 12-in. piece of clear cedar (requiring no gluing or assembly of boards, merely the cutting out of the shape from a single piece of wood).

- Third, both shapes were drawn on the computer and cut using full-scale print-outs as templates, thus minimizing layout time.

These elements provide a little magic amid all the shingles.

adaptation of those techniques to create a house that steps from one story to a story and a half to a full three-story tower and back down again, with its plan cranked at an angle to accommodate the multiple views presented by the river. Even when building with generic materials, this level of complexity needs a clearheaded can-do builder, and the owners found one in Matt Fogarty, who combined enthusiasm and skill to bring the project in on budget.

CUSTOM FIT

The floor plan was precisely laid out to fit the way the family uses the house. To the south, the master bedroom enjoys full sunlight and projects into the backyard to receive wonderful down-river views. The central portion of the first floor is given over to the public areas of TV room, office, and dining room, with

● ● ● **TERRACE VIEW.** Windows, site development, and house shape all conspire to give the back side of the house an embracing view of the river beyond, while showing how standard parts can be gently animated if you know how to detail them. [above]

FRONT ENTRY. The front door is nestled under a large shed roof overhang below the dominant tower and flanked by an expressive tree-like column. [top, facing page]

ART LOFT. Skylights, windows, and soaring roof lines surround an out-of-the-way perch for the owner's artistic endeavors. [bottom, facing page]

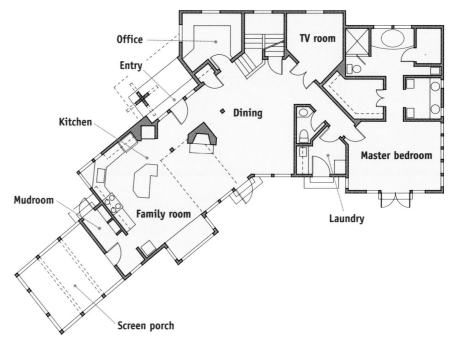

● ●● **STOCK STAIR.** Built of stock parts, the stair gently meanders up to the second floor, creating a shelf to the upper left and serving to illuminate the upstairs hall and the deep first-floor interior below.

FIRST-FLOOR PLAN

The footprint of the house is angled to capture views of the river. A separate master bedroom suite receives southerly light and is separated from the public spaces of the house by the minicorridor formed by the walk-in closet and the half-bath/laundry.

SECOND-FLOOR PLAN

The stair provides access to two bedrooms, a common bath, and a loft space used as a small art studio. The two dormers on the street side are used as sitting and dressing spaces.

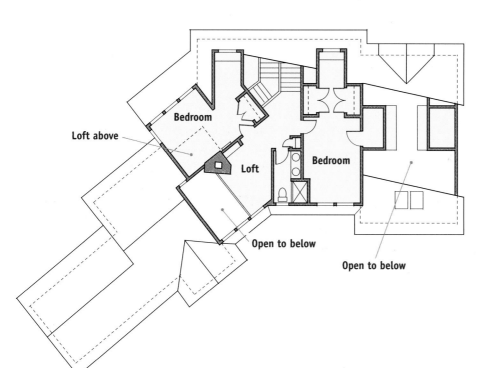

kitchen and family room occupying the angled wing that looks to the cross-river views, and a screen porch at the shady northerly tip of the house that faces up-river views. The front door is located in the New England center-hall tradition, opening directly onto the back of the central hearth. Springing up from the front door is the most dramatic three-dimensional element of the house: the tower entry, which contains a bedroom and clerestory loft space.

Ceilings ascend to take advantage of the many roof forms in the house. The master bedroom suite enjoys a full cathedral ceiling with the master bath completely open and accessible to the sleeping area (another owner-specific requirement). The central hearth sits within a portion of the soaring two-and-a-half story tower space, which also uses skylights to draw light down into a second-floor studio balcony for the resident artist.

COLOR AND DETAIL

Color is used to focus attention outside and highlight interior spaces. On the exterior, high-quality stock windows have a factory-applied deep green paint, a color that was repeated on the column set at the front door. For exterior trim, the owners opted for the simplest of all solutions—no applied trim. Not only did this save money, it happily reflected the owners' desire for a simple, clean, New England countenance.

On the inside, one of the owner fully engaged her creative palette to create multiple experiences of color. Deep tones in

●●● **BEDROOM NOOK.** Two street-facing "doghouse" dormers not only provide light and air but also create the sort of intimate space that's perfect for a bedroom. [above]

LOFT BEDROOM. Rather than use the loft for sleeping, it becomes a private refuge for a teenage daughter whose passion for popular culture is plainly evident. [above left]

intimate bedroom spaces make personal statements, while lighter contrasting tones call out various wall and ceiling planes throughout the house.

The doors are solid-core smooth-skin formed composite wood, which don't warp, present superior sound-deadening characteristics, and save money over their solid wood counterparts. All interior trim was clear flat stock with full 1-in.-thick lintels (the top horizontal pieces) set to lightly project beyond the other ¾-in.-thick elements employed. Floors are primarily standard 2¼-in. strip oak, with some tiled areas.

Not every choice was based on saving money. The owners opted to have a traditional masonry fireplace, which costs more than its prefab metal equivalent but kept costs down by using drywall and sheet-stock wainscoting for most of its interior surfacing. History was brought into the home by recycling three old quarried stones found on the site as hearth framing pieces. The stair (constructed of standard parts) is strategically located in the middle of the house to serve as a lightwell and as a natural separation between the two second-floor bedrooms.

When you know your life is going to change, you can either embrace that change or resist it, trying to force-fit old accommodations to new needs. In this case, the owners had the vision to understand that lives do inevitably evolve, and they had the courage to reflect that change in their new home. In so doing, they capitalized on a fairly substantial net cash benefit by selling a nicely renovated traditional suburban house in a good neighborhood and building a smaller, carefully detailed replacement virtually down the street.

MASTER BEDROOM. A big part of the appeal of master-bedroom-down houses is that they have direct access to the outside. Here, stock windows were positioned to accommodate the headboard of the bed and capture southern light, while the skylights above prevent glare and give some backlighting.

BAY WATCH. Originally planned as a spot for informal dining, the bay window has such an exquisite view that the owners decided to use it as a sitting area that could be enjoyed at any time of day, not just at mealtimes. [left]

MASTER BATH. A tall small space is enhanced by the deep hue of the ceiling. The niches (left and right) were sized to perfectly accommodate the owner's plants and knickknacks. [below]

FAMILY ROOM. The masonry fireplace, which provides a solid center point to the double-height space, is built with stones recycled from the property.

THREE-PART HARMONY. As seen from the street, the lightness of the pink shed (right) contrasts with the solidity of the main bedroom/dining room form (left) and the ascending stair tower (center). Materials, colors, and shapes are all different, yet they are coordinated in their stark simplicity.

The Houses Built for You

THE SPEC DEVELOPMENTS THAT DOMINATE THE HOUSING MARKET offer little to people who want their homes to reflect their personal values. If the misfit is grave enough and the homeowners care enough, this can mean either renovating an existing home or building from scratch—options that are time-consuming and financially less certain than buying a new house. However, there are now alternatives for those who can't accept these housing options. While this book focuses on individuals who've doggedly pursued their vision by building their own home because they could not find it anywhere else, isolated spec projects are beginning to appear that reflect the ability of the housing market to address a new type of homebuyer. These "square-peg" homebuyers don't easily fit into the round-hole solutions that are predominantly offered up in the marketplace.

This last project presents an alternative to building your own home that still allows for personal expression while offering the quicker gratification and financial security of an already-built home. Prospect, a housing development in Longmont, Colorado, offers sites for about 270 idiosyncratic architect-designed houses

Traditional Neighborhood Design

TRADITIONAL NEIGHBORHOOD DESIGN has long been advocated by Andres Duany and Elizabeth Plater-Zyberk, who created the movement's signature community in Seaside, Florida, in the early 1980s. What distinguishes TND communities from their midcentury housing development predecessors is the emphasis on pedestrian activity, mixed use (homes, rentals, offices, and businesses all set together), and a town planning layout that conveys the essence of what makes small-town America so sentimentally appealing.

As with many of these projects, the community shown here has multiple miniparks, broad boulevards, back alleys for parking, house locations that are located tight to the street, specific height requirements (both minimum and maximum), and a tree-lined streetscape enlivened by the homes' porches and expressive entryways. All these requirements intentionally try to recreate the ambience of a late-19th- or early-20th-century American "home town."

(combined with about 50 places of business). Although a few of the homes in this community are custom designed for individual clients, the central premise of the development is spec-built homes. But unlike most run-of-the-mill spec developments, the homes in Prospect have a definite aesthetic edge to them geared to the atypical housing consumer who's looking for a home that defies the round-hole definitions of Cape, colonial, and ranch.

MID-COURSE CORRECTION

Usually it takes a single person to push forward an idea that on the surface seems ill advised. In 1994, developer Kiki Wallace saw his native Colorado beset with sprawling, artless development. He bought a 77-acre tree farm near the center of Longmont, a classic late-20th-century town with rapidly diminishing farmland, a "miracle mile" of national chain stores, and the odd remnant farm all set amid a sea of high-density, nondescript spec housing developments. Wallace decided to engage the services of a design team who had been instrumental in reinventing community development, Andres Duany and Elizabeth Plater-Zyberk (see the sidebar at left).

As with most Traditional Neighborhood Design developments, a designated group of architects designed each building with traditional architecture as the model. The architects worked for individual builders who bought lots on spec. The first 60 houses of the development sold rapidly, which would make most developers quite happy. But Kiki Wallace was not satisfied.

Total Development Site Size:	**77 Acres** (6.1 acres open space/park planned)
Number of Detached Residential Houses:	177
Number of Attached Houses:	92
Number of Mixed Use Housing/Offices:	43
Number of Work Spaces:	12
Price Range:	Purchase price starting at $300,000 (land and house)
Typical Lot Size:	¹⁄₁₀ acre up to ¹⁄₆ acre for detached house

CONTEXT. Although the buildings along this street boast a variety of colors, materials, and styles, the consistent shapes and simple detailing create a sense of community amid the stylistic expression. [left]

FRONT VIEW. The bold colors of the roof overhang, balcony, and porch, along with the playful arrangement of the windows, add plenty of exterior seasoning. The long wing of the house forms and shields a terrace from the alleyway that provides access for cars to the garages in back. [below]

SITE PLAN. Prospect has a wide variety of potential for different types of occupancy. This color-coded plan shows sites for single-family homes in gray, attached parks/civic amenities in aqua, commercial buildings in yellow, high-density apartments in red, and mixed use in other colors. [left]

Windows: A Key to a Home's Identity

ALONG WITH ALL THE CLASSIC Traditional Neighborhood Design criteria concerning the house's shape, its position on the building lot, and the materials used (in Prospect's case, a fairly open-ended list), this particular development has some extraordinary "rules" for windows. These include:

- No more than 40 percent of the area of any front façade of a house should be made up of windows.

- Windows (except by special exception) need to be at least one-and-a-half times as tall as they are wide.

- The mullions between windows need to be at least 4 in. wide.

- Windows need to be either painted wood or clear-finished metal.

- Any window that exceeds 2 ft. in size in any direction needs to have a muntin (a grill pattern) applied to it.

These simplified rules help to unify a potentially chaotic group of houses, even though these regulations are proportional rather than stylistic.

Wallace began to see the folly of making an architectural theme park in a part of the world where there were precious few of the historic precedents typically applied to TND communities. He hired Mark Sofield, a young Yale-educated architect, to devise a way to redirect the entire project. What has evolved is a dynamic partnership between the visionary (Wallace) and the innovative advocate (Sofield). Between the two of them, they shifted the course of Prospect by creating a simple set of design regulations, not only providing a way for all projects to be responsive to the streetscape issues of scale, detail, and massing that Duany and Plater-Zyberk so fervently advocate, but also creating houses that are designed for people who want a very personalized house.

SPICE AMID THE VANILLA

The proof that this development is not some elitist fantasy is the fact that the houses sell well. Even though each builder pays for each home's unique design and it takes more time, energy, and thought to build them, the typical price for one of these homes is only about 10 percent higher than one of its predictable neighboring counterparts in a mostly vanilla housing market. Despite this higher cost, returns of almost 100 percent increase in value over three or four years are not uncommon.

Color doesn't have to be limited to interior design.

● ● ● **A MIX THAT WORKS.** By maintaining continuity of scale along the street, variations of shape and detail can be combined with color without creating chaos in the community.

A SENSE OF HOME. Fences, porches, and distinctive elements like this miniature tower create a sense of personalized scale that helps temper the expressive aesthetics of the development, giving these houses a more residential character. [top]

COLOR CODED. When intense colors are used consistently, their overall impact is woven into the fabric of the community. [above]
●
●
●

● ● ● **FLYAWAY HOME.** Nicknamed "The Butterfly House" for its roofs that pitch inward, this home (designed by Hobbs Design) has a classic "L" configuration, with a combined garage and studio set to the rear. Simple colors as well as the straightforward arrangement of windows are used to reinforce the various components of the house. (The interior of the house is shown on the facing page.)

An inspection of the competition shows why personalized expression in home design is a virtual requirement for a certain sector of the housing market. One neighborhood adjacent to Prospect has a palette of three or four different tones of brown and gray with all roofs having the exact same pitch and form, while another development features a classic mid-20th-century ranch neighborhood, and yet another is a Disneyesque reinterpretation of the bungalow.

It could be said that all housing designs are balancing acts between giving enough of the familiar and comfortable that owners can honestly feel that they are at home in the house they buy and at the same time offering up the excitement and energizing expression that makes them feel that their home is alive and reflects who they are. This dance between the safe and the exciting is the essence of Prospect. An unintended consequence is that the earlier, more traditional homes in the development have gained a stature in contrast to their livelier counterparts that they didn't have before. The following pages will focus on one of these houses, designed by out-of-state architects Terra Firma, Inc., that is both affordable and inspiring.

●●● **MAKING CONNECTIONS.** The stair located at the joint between the long and short legs of the "L" creates a central two-story area in a house that otherwise isolates both floors from each other. As with many Prospect homes, the interiors are simple drywall and flat casing trim.

Spec House Solar

Not unlike Prospect itself, this house breaks many of the accepted rules. Whereas predictable aesthetics are usually the norm in the world of speculative development, this home has the sort of custom touches, features, and shapes associated with a particular client's direct input into the design process. Here, however, the client bought a design that the architects of Terra Firma, Inc., (Danny Sagan and Alisa Dworsky) had already created. The design was intentionally exuberant, while reflecting a fundamental commitment to passive solar design principles and energy efficiency. (The architects are from Vermont, a state where passive solar design can be found even in spec houses.)

Because of the design's commitment to solar design, the home's main spaces have a large number of windows facing directly south, with a concrete floor designed to retain heat gained from the winter sun. Additionally, there's a wood stove to provide nighttime heating, and the staircase serves as a virtual flue to funnel sun- or wood-heated air to the bedrooms above. Perhaps this home's best energy-conserving device is its tight design. The main house is a two-bedroom house of only 1,200 sq. ft., with a separate apartment over the detached garage.

The home's simple layout is brought to life by the way its rooms reveal themselves on the exterior. The common living room is a skewed one-story box, while the bedrooms are built as a house within a house, with their own timber structure system that supports the sleeping spaces above the dining space. The bathrooms are stacked to form a two-story tower, and the stairs have their own shed roof set to the back of the lofted bedrooms. A low covered porch wraps around the bath tower. Where bedrooms above and living space below overlap, a dining space is defined by the timber columns needed to support the second floor. There are almost no walls on the first floor save those that separate the bathroom from the back door. The home's first floor spreads out to include a covered porch on one side and a sun porch on the other.

Location:	Longmont, Colorado
Year Built:	2000
Architect:	Terra Firma, Inc. (Danny Sagan and Alisa Dworsky)
Finished Heated Space:	1,280 sq. ft. house, 440 sq. ft. apartment over garage
Costs:	Project Budget—$210,000 Site Development—$15,000 Design Fee—$8,000

●●● **BEDROOMS WITH A CURVE.** The big design move on the exterior is the curved roof over the bedrooms, which was formed by having 2x dimensional lumber span in the short direction from wall to wall, a distance of only 13 ft.

HOUSE WITHIN A HOUSE. The dominant element on the interior is an exposed column-and-beam substructure that sits at the core of the house, independently supporting the bedrooms above. This central house within a house connects stair, entry, kitchen, and living spaces and defines the dining space within an open floor plan. [facing page]

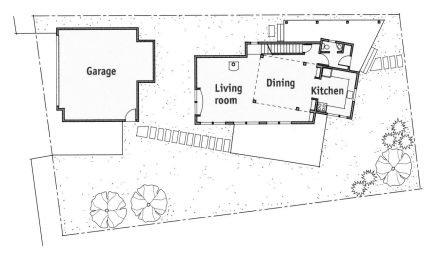

FIRST-FLOOR PLAN

The house is formed of four basic parts: the main one-story living space, the kitchen and dining block, the porch, and the bedrooms upstairs. The separate garage is accessed from a back alley, typical of Traditional Neighborhood Design developments.

Garage

Living room

Dining

Kitchen

When a home's plan determines its shape, it can save space (and money).

Color, This Time on the Outside

MANY OF THE HOUSES IN THIS BOOK USE COLOR to great effect on their interiors. Most of the houses in Prospect use it to equal effect on their exteriors. The home shown here has a curved-top bedroom block painted a deep greenish-gray, while the bathroom tower is clad in a lighter gray vertical siding, and the lean-to at the rear is a pale yellow. Trim transitions from pale pinky peach in some places to muted gray-green for the doors, in response to the various parts and shapes of the house. Careful use of color can make a house come alive, but controlling the intensity and tone can make one home out of many colors.

BUDGET MATTERS

Costs for building this home were kept down a number of ways. Standard materials are used throughout (windows, siding, trim, and so on); a straight-run, closed-stringer stock stair saves money over its more customized counterpart; and a slab-on-grade first floor is inherently cheaper than either a crawl space or a full basement. Kitchen cabinets are off the rack, and all interior surfaces (except for the timber structure) are painted drywall. Roofs are standard standing-seam aluminum. The simple second-floor bedrooms are identical in size, allowing for multiple family-use patterns.

On a site that is scarcely ⅛ acre, this 1,200-sq.-ft. house and its 20-ft. by 20-ft. two-story outbuilding present seven distinct forms and almost as many approaches to siding, roofing, and color, making the small elaborate without expensive detailing. By using flat stock trim throughout and by consciously keeping the eaves, shapes, and planes unaligned, the exterior of the house is aesthetically consistent despite all the different shapes and surfaces. A loose choreography between the pieces of this ensemble makes for a happy dance of architectural parts.

Sometimes homes have their own unique identity, no matter who the occupant is. In this particular case, a design that the architects hoped could be applied anywhere by anyone who was interested in passive solar techniques and affordable construction found a home in Colorado. Unmistakably dynamic, the end result is incontrovertibly domestic and perfectly reflects the innovative spirit of a Traditional Neighborhood Design community that is anything but predictable.

● ● ● **MASTER BEDROOM.** Set on the second floor of the two-story portion of the house, corner windows and a vaulted ceiling create a safe harbor for the room's ultimate focal point—the bed.

DINING ROOM/KITCHEN. The coffered ceiling, space-defining wood flooring, end window, built-ins, and kitchen cabinets all reinforce this space as the centered heart of the home from which all the shapes and colors radiate. [above]

SWEET DREAMS. The diagonal flooring, pocket windows, and vaulted roof provide a distinctive setting for this nursery. [left]

Architects and Designers

Peter Q. Bohlin
Bohlin Cywinski Jackson
8 West Market Street
Suite 1200
Wilkes-Barre, PA 18701
(570) 825-8756
www.bcj.com
Pages: 112-121

Brian Brand,
Baylis Architects
10801 Main Street
Suite 110
Bellevue, WA 98004
(425) 454-0566
www.baylisarchitects.com
Pages: 26-35, 84-93 (with architect Ed Sozinho)

Turner Brooks, Eeva Pelkonen
Turner Brooks Architects
319 Peck Street
New Haven, CT 06513
(203) 772-3244
www.turnerbrooksarchitect.com
Pages: 94-101

Burr and McCallum Architects
720 Main Street
P.O. Box 345
Williamstown, MA 01267
(413) 458-2121
www.burrandmccallum.com
Pages: 46-55

John J. Casbarian and Danny Samuels
Taft Architects
2370 Rice Boulevard
Suite 112
Houston, TX 77005
(713) 522-2988
Pages: 56-65

Ross Chapin
Ross Chapin Architects
P.O. Box 230
Langley, WA 98260
(360) 221 2373
www.rosschapin.com
Pages: 36-45

Alfredo De Vido
Alfredo De Vido Architects
412 East 85th Street
New York, NY 10028
(212) 517-6100
www.devido-architects.com
Pages: 132-139

Duo Dickinson, AIA
Duo Dickinson, Architect
94 Bradley Road
Madison, CT 06443
(203) 245-0405
www.duodickinson.com
Pages: 66-73, 122-131, 180-189

Bret Drager
Drager Gould Architects
625 South Commerce Street
Suite 310
Tacoma, WA 98402
(253) 761-3650
www.dragergould.com
Pages: 74-83

Wayne L. Good, FAIA
Good Architecture
132 West Street, Suite A
Annapolis, MD 21401
(410) 268-7414
Pages: 102-111

Kimble Hobbs, AIA, NCARB
Hobbs Design
325 20th Street
Boulder, CO 80302
(303) 444-5508
www.hobbsdesign.com
Pages: 196-197

Charles G. Mueller, AIA
Centerbrook Architects & Planners
67 Main Street
P.O. Box 955
Centerbrook, CT 06409
(860) 767-0175
www.centerbrook.com
Pages: 16-25

James Mary O'Connor
Moore Ruble Yudell
933 Pico Boulevard
Santa Monica, CA 90405
(310) 450-1400
www.moorerubleyudell.com
Pages: 140-149

Wellington Reiter
Urban Instruments
424 Newtonville Avenue
Newton, MA 02460
(617) 559-0502
www.urbaninstruments.com
Pages: 150-159

Lori Ryker
Ryker/Nave Design
13 Cokedale Spur Road
Livingston, MT 59047
(406) 222-7488
www.rykernave.com
Pages: 160-169

Richard Shugar
Shugar Architecture
225 West 5th Street
Eugene, OR 97401
(541) 521-2728
www.shugararchitecture.com
Pages: 170-179

Daniel Sagan and Alisa Dworsky
Terra Firma, Inc.
P.O. Box I
Randolph, VT 05060
(802) 728-6401
Pages: 198-201

Mark Sofield, Designer
1813 South Coffman
Longmont, CO 80501
(303) 776-4607
Pages: 190-195